IT TAKES 2:
WHO IS HELPING YOU LEAD?

Ramone Harper
FOREWORD FROM DR. DHARIUS DANIELS

Published in Nashville, Tennessee, by Heritage Publishing

Library of Congress Cataloging-in-Publishing   2017942270

ISBN   9781732072206

TABLE OF CONTENTS

FOREWORD

Joseph is one of my favorite biblical characters. His life story is recorded in the Old Testament. He was creative, visionary, strategic, grounded, and wise. His strategic leadership and business acumen not only positioned the Egyptian government to prosper during an economic downturn, it also spared the life of his family, who happened to be God's chosen people.

I believe the genius of it all is that Joseph did this sitting in the "second chair." He didn't occupy the role of a senior leader but accomplished more, impacted more, and experienced more than many senior leaders will in their lifetime. His life and ministry are a profound picture of the power of the "two." He had no ambition for other roles and made no attempts to occupy them. He simply bloomed where he was planted; and as a result, God's kingdom was expanded, his family was provided for, and God got the glory.

In an era of unprecedented exposure to the accomplishments of others, many leaders have become confused about their assignments. It is as if this exposure has created an appetite of ambition that often undervalues the power of finding their lane, living in their lane, and loving their lane. This is what this amazing book is about. This work reminds the Josephs of the world that your contribution to businesses, churches, and government is invaluable. You are a gift to the world and a special gift to people like me.

I've had the blessing and privilege of having Ramone Harper as a Joseph for over a decade. My life and our organization would not be the same without him. The content contained in these pages isn't just a message he has written; it's a message he has lived. May the words on these pages bless you the way his life and service have blessed me.

Dr. Dharius Daniels
Senior Leader, Change Church

ENDORSEMENTS

For many years now, Ramone Harper has used his unique skill set and spiritual gifts to help pastors transform their congregations. He has mastered the art of helping pastors build infrastructure for their vision. As you read his work, you will gain valuable insights into what it takes to make vision work. In fact, you will discover "It Takes 2!"

Bishop Walter S. Thomas
Senior Pastor, New Psalmist Baptist Church

I have had the distinct pleasure to serve and work alongside Ramone for over eight years. His ministry and consulting business have flourished because he always puts the needs of others first. I'm a firm believer in Ecclesiastes 4:9-10 (NIV): "Two are better than one, because they have a good return for their labor: If either of them falls down, one can help the other up." This book speaks to that. It is with great enthusiasm that I recommend *It Takes 2*. Your ministry or organization will thank you.

Mike Regina
Principal, Big Sky Enterprises

This book is a must-read because smart leaders are surrounded by smarter people. You will discover how to have the right people on your team to make the vision a reality. This book will help you identify key people who will help you and your organization make a greater impact.

Tim DeTellis
President, New Missions

As a former #1 professional athlete and a current #1 in my home and business, I can definitely testify about the importance of the #2. I played running back for a D1 SEC school and then started for the Pittsburgh Steelers as a rookie after being drafted seventh overall in the 1989 NFL Draft. At the University of Georgia, there was no way I was getting in the end zone without my #2s: my fullback and my offensive line. With the Steelers, it was my fullback, Merril Hoge, and my O-line who plowed the ground I was able to trample.

As a husband, professional speaker, and leadership development consultant, my role is out front and, often, standing on a stage holding a microphone. But without my #2, my wife and business partner, nothing gets scheduled on my calendar, invoices don't go out, keynote speech notes don't get typed, and our business doesn't get marketed. It's the #2s in my life who have made it possible for me to have any measure of success, and I'm so grateful to Ramone for bringing attention to these overlooked, unsung heroes. What Ramone is contributing to every kind of leadership through this book isn't just enlightening, it's essential.

Tim Worley
Co-Founder | CEO, Worley Global Enterprises
Former Running Back, University of Georgia Bulldogs
and the Pittsburgh Steelers

As the former mayor of Westampton Township, New Jersey, I was always uniquely aware that any growth or positive advancement of our community would advance by the power of "we." Almost every imaginable vision or plan that I've been involved in, officially and unofficially, has been the result of sharing the destiny of the collective with a clear understanding of having achieved a measure of buy-in by being inclusive.

A poem by John Donne has always resonated with me as a leader: "No man is an island, entire of itself; every man is a piece of the continent, a part of the main." I would like to congratulate and thank Pastor Ramone Harper on his newest tome, *It Takes 2: Who Is Helping You Lead?* which stands as a guidepost for the notion of "we" in a "me" world. Continued blessings and success!

C. Andre' Daniels
Mayor Emeritus, Westampton Township, New Jersey

The word *vice* is one of only about 500 words in the English language with more than three distinct meanings. It could mean an addiction to something or a leader who is second-in-command. What if both of the top two ways the word is used most were combined in one? That's Ramone.

Ramone's passion for (or addiction to) and experience (2man for 20+ years) with being a kingmaker has contributed to the world's shift in all things aligned with God's glory in this digital age. This literary piece has inspired and enlightened me and will inspire and enlighten you to lift your selfless acts toward your quest for God's purpose in your life!

Marc P. Desgraves, CPA
"Vice" President, Turning Dreams Into Realities Scholarship
and Mentorship Program

Great leaders inspire others to serve alongside them while learning to become great leaders. For those aspiring to become great leaders, this book is an awesome tool to use when starting or while continuing on the path toward great leadership. *It Takes Two: Who Is Helping You Lead?* can be used as a blueprint for building strong and healthy relationships between senior leaders and support teams. Ramone Harper has done an exceptional job in explaining the importance of supporting a senior leader while "embracing [a] uniqueness in helping lead . . . from the second, third, or fourth chair." This book should be part of every leader's library and used as a reference guide for leadership development.

Elder Derrick Noble
Chief of Staff to the Presiding Bishop, Full Gospel Baptist
Fellowship International

11

Over my professional career, I've worked in a major professional services firm and a Fortune 500 corporation with global operations all over the world. In both environments, I've observed many times that our top and most successful executives were always supported by the best and brightest people. Those same executives would also tell you that they couldn't do what they do without their number 2 (or 3). I think this book relays the importance of a top-level support team and puts their contributions in perspective

Terrance Turner
Vice President, Finance, Electronics, and Solutions,
Emerson Commercial and Residential Solutions

As a second-in-command, you must be able to lead and follow in the same space. The lion and the lamb must live inside the soul of the second-in-command. The boldness of a lion will be required to lead effectively, and yet the humility of the lamb is essential to understand the people you are leading. If you are a second-in-command, this book is for you!

Abram Gomez
Executive Pastor, Cross Church

An absolute must-read for every leader and their support person or team! *It Takes Two* breaks down what leadership is all about: understanding your role as a leader and understanding the importance of having a strong team to help you deliver, execute, and implement the vision. And if you're a support team member, this book will help you understand how important your role is to an organization's success.

Shontaye Hawkins, MBA
CEO and Founder,
Profit Is the New Black®

WORDS OF WISDOM FROM ESTABLISHED 2S

"A lot of men and women don't last long in these positions because of stress, burnout, lack of appreciation, and because they are no longer graced for the assignment."

Elder Derrick Noble
Chief of Staff, Full Gospel Baptist Fellowship International
Presiding Bishop Joseph W. Walker III

Note: Elder Noble has served in his current role for a little over three years but was previously COO for almost ten years before. Almost 28 years ago, he left corporate America and began serving in full-time ministry as executive administrator for Bishop Clarence E. McClendon at the Church of the Harvest, Los Angeles, California.

"Pastor Chris was my youth pastor 28 years ago in my hometown of Colorado Springs. When he planted Highlands 16 years ago, I moved to Birmingham to be the first staff member. A 2 is a son or daughter of the house. As a son, you think, act, and speak like an heir. I do a teaching that lists the qualities of being a son."

Layne Shranz
Associate Pastor, Church of the Highlands,
Pastor Chris Hodges

"My advice to a new 2 coming into the role is to ask yourself these questions: Can I work with a few? Can I walk in the night season? Can I walk while my leader rides? Can I walk with them when unsure of directions? Can I walk with them while being ridiculed? Can I be motivated to work with rubbish? Can I walk with them when they don't disclose the directions?"

Pastor Lawrence Robinson
The Potters House,
Bishop T. D. Jakes

Note: Pastor Robinson has served with Bishop Jakes for over 40 years.

"I balance ministry and family life by preparing in advance with scheduling, organization, and delegation. I consciously make an effort to be present when I am with my family instead of taking work home as I did in the past."

Cheryletta "C. C." Harrison, COO
The City of Love Church
Bishop Lester Love

Note: C. C. has served in her current capacity for approximately seven years but has served under Bishop Love for over 17 years.

"I am not sure what type of training a 2 needs as much as connections with people in the same position. Pastors are different, but they are also very similar. Having people to bounce things off of or sometimes vent to is healthy."

Phil Clemens
Executive Global Operations Pastor and Campus Pastor
of Weldon Spring Campus, Faith Church, Pastors David
and Nicole Crank

Note: Phil has served in this capacity for approximately five years but has been connected to his leaders for almost 18 years in different capacities.

"Over eight years ago, I transitioned from planting my own church in Fresno, Texas. I dissolved Great Expectations Christian Church to accept the newly created executive pastor's position at Fallbrook Church. My word of advice that I would give to a spouse of a 2 is to understand that the whole church is now part of your family. You have to be prepared to share your husband or wife with others, many of whom you may never come to know personally. Be prepared for sacrifice."

Pastor Olus Holder Jr.
Executive Pastor, Fallbrook Church
Pastor Michael A. Pender Sr.

"My advice for a new 2 coming into the role is to understand that there are ALWAYS 1,000 reasons why something won't work. Find the one way it can. God deserves our ingenuity, creativity, and relentless pursuit of His heart. Don't let your comfort become 'brakes' that slow down God's work."

Corbett Drew
Executive Director, Venue Church
Pastor Tavner Smith

Note: Corbett has served in this capacity for less than two years but has been a volunteer/friend/advisor since the church was preparing to launch in 2013.

"Positional placement does not determine Kingdom effectiveness. In the case of Joseph, it is proven that a person can be influential and effective wherever God places them." (from his book *12 Lessons From the Second Chariot: Leading Where You Are*)

Abram Gomez
Executive Pastor, Cross Church

Initially hired on staff as pastoral assistant, Jeff Smith assisted the senior pastor, associate pastor, and the pastoral care pastor before becoming the director of their network. He has since been named as lead pastor in Fredericksburg, Virginia. He attributes his longevity (23 years) to "trusting God's placement and timing for my life. Have other things you are growing in and involved with. This helps you not to define yourself by your role." His advice to someone new coming into the role of a 2man is "to have confidence that serving as a 2 is your assignment."

Jeff Smith
Lead Pastor of Strong Tower and
Director of Cornerstone Global Network
Bishop Michael Pitts

INTRODUCTION

"It takes 2 to make a thing go right!
It takes 2 to make it out of sight!"[1]

Those lyrics are from a 1988 Top 40 platinum-selling song by Rob Base and DJ E-Z Rock, who initially made the song with samples from another song written in 1972 by James Brown and performed by Lyn Collins called "Think (About It)." These lyrics succinctly sum up my convictions as an executive leader. Over the last 20 years, I have served in various executive leadership positions from the federal government to the nonprofit sector to the corporate world, and I felt the need to share experiences—mine and those of others—that have contributed to the success of those organizations.

In 2006, I talked with Odell Dickerson and Derrick Noble about the need for developing resources to help train and encourage people who serve in roles similar to theirs because there wasn't much material out there. We also noticed how many secondary leaders lacked the training, support, and resources to help them be successful in their unique position. Most conferences and books are targeted to senior leaders but not to the executive support leadership staff.

Along the journey, I saw great executive support leaders help lead the companies that they worked for, experience the best that life has to offer, and make major impact without having to be impressive. They were some of the greatest leaders, creative minds, innovators, and game-changers that I had met. The world has felt their impact but just may not have known their names.

But when I went back to learn from these leaders and to be enamored by their work, in most cases, I discovered that they were no longer serving in those positions. Instead, they had transitioned to what they perceived as a promotion or an elevation of sorts. Yes, you guessed it. They had left the #2 seat in order to become a #1;

and, sadly, in more than 90 percent of those cases, they have never been heard of again.

I am a firm believer that it does take two (and three and four and more) to make things go right in an organization. Whether in the corporate world, the religious sector, nonprofit organizations, government, sports, or entertainment, no one man or woman can build a winning tradition without help.

Tell me about a Steve Jobs, and I can show you a Steve Wozniak. Show me a Bishop T. D. Jakes, and I can introduce you to a Pastor Lawrence Robinson. Explain to me the magnitude of the Civil Rights Movement lead by Dr. Martin Luther King Jr., and I can talk to you about Dr. Ralph Abernathy and Bayard Rustin. Brag about the greatness of President Abraham Lincoln, and I would dare you to research William Seward. If the greatest basketball player of all times is Michael Jordan, then I would say he never won a ring until Scottie Pippen matured as his sidekick. You love Jerry Lewis, but I respect Dean Martin. Get the picture? It may take one to lead a great organization, but it takes two to make it out of sight.

My objective in writing this book is a dual one. I want to help senior leaders (whom I refer to as 1s) understand the need for having quality executive support leaders on their team and how to find them. And I want to inspire and encourage those who serve in executive leadership support roles (whom I affectionately refer to as 2men, or 2s) to embrace their uniqueness in helping lead their organizations from the second, third, or fourth chair. I am motivated because I am tired of seeing great 2s leave their posts to become ordinary 1s.

I want to thank my pastor, Dr. Dharius Daniels, for his support, motivation, and contributions to this book. In March 2017, he told me that it was time to start developing a network where I could pour into others who serve in similar roles as I do, and he recommended that we collaborate and write this book about the value of 2men and 2women.

I also want to thank my wife, Verily, and my amazing children (Ilexuz, Amari, Raven, Zi'yhon, and the young prince Deon) for their contributions to my career and to this book because they have lived and experienced the unique ride that comes while riding in the second chariot. Verily, who is a licensed professional counselor, contributed to the writing and development of this book, especially to the chapters dealing with challenges and family life.

Finally, I want to thank the amazing 2men who allowed me to interview them and get their insight while doing my writing research. I am humbled and honored that they would take the time to hear my vision and share their insight and wisdom to help develop this book as they provide diverse high-level executive support to their 1s. I look forward to introducing them to the world and to them sharing their wisdom and experience with my network.

---

[1] "It Takes 2," written by Robert Ginyard, performed by Rob Base and DJ E-Z Rock, from the album *It Takes Two* (Profile Records, August 1988

WHAT IS A 2MAN?

Nobody remembers who came in second place. Who lost to the Dallas Cowboys during the years when The Big Three (Troy Aikman, Emmitt Smith, and Michael Irvin) won the Super Bowl in 1993, 1994, and 1996? Who did Michael Phelps beat on his way to winning an Olympic-record 18 gold medals? Who won second at the 2017 Kentucky Derby when Always Dreaming finished in first place? Most people don't know, and most of them don't care.

That case is sometimes made when discussing 2men. Nobody wants to come in second, so the concept of raising up and developing 2s becomes even more challenging. But it is necessary because everyone can't be "The Man," or a 1. And the sooner we teach that it's OK to be the man or the woman next to "The Man," then we can increase productivity and decrease esteem and worthiness issues.

But the dynamics between 1s and 2s are all about perspective. The 1s and 2s aren't in competition. Instead, they are actually playing for the same goal. If asked who helped Michael Jordan win six championship rings, most people would say Scottie Pippen because he couldn't win without him. Troy Aikman needed Emmitt Smith. Muhammad Ali had Angelo Dundee, his trainer and consultant, in his corner.

It is crucial to see the role of the 2man through the lens of partnership. The people on a support team are essential to the mission of the organization and are the difference between a pretty good team and a world championship team. They are the best at what they do, and they allow the Jordans of ministry and corporate America to take the last shot at the end of the game, get the MVP, and do the interviews. They are the ones who make the crucial assist, get that tough rebound, and set the timely screen to free up the Jordans for the game-winning shot.

Members of a support staff don't get the recognition, but they share the same trophy, get championship rings, and cash their bonus checks. They ride on the same parade float, and some of them even get a few minutes to share their experiences with the crowd. They are all on the same team as the 1s and have learned how to play their role for the overall benefit of the organization.

I am reminded of my favorite basketball team, the Detroit "Bad Boys" Pistons of the 1980s. My favorite player was the star and the undoubted leader, Isiah Thomas, who was the point guard, or the 1. But the Pistons also had a 2 in a guard named Joe Dumars, who was just as instrumental to them winning back-to-back championships as anyone else.

Since Dumars was a 2, he didn't have the same leadership responsibilities as Thomas, but he was a silent assassin. Occasionally, though, when Thomas needed a break, Dumars would step up and run the 1-spot until Thomas was ready to come back into the game. Dumars was versatile and could play any role that Thomas needed him to play, whether that was to relieve him temporarily of leadership duties, play defense on the other team's best player, do the dirty work, or occasionally become the leading scorer.

In the 1990 NBA finals, Dumars played so well that he won the MVP of the finals. Thomas was happy for him and valued him as a 2, and that made Dumars play that much harder and respect Thomas even more as his #1. You would have to understand Dumars's character in order to see that he didn't like the spotlight and didn't need it to perform. He just wanted to win.

This is the right mindset for 2s to have in order to be successful in their positions. We should be confident in our abilities, but we should also be willing to defer to the 1s so that together we can win championships. As 2s, we must be content when we're not called to the podium to speak to the media and get all the accolades. Instead, we should just do our jobs in excellence, and we will get a ring, too. I am a living witness!

I have served as a 2man for my entire professional career, dating back to my first job as a management analyst for the federal government. But, actually, I probably started on my path as a 2 long before then.

Growing up, I served as the consultant/advisor to my group of friends and basketball teammates. I wasn't the toughest kid, the most vocal leader, the best player, or the most flamboyant on the team; but I was always the one to whom my friends and teammates could come for advice or just to bounce off their ideas before they made big decisions. They had to speak to the strategist, me, first to make sure their childish schemes would work. If not, they had to come up with a plan that would work before they went live.

On the varsity basketball team, I was named co-captain. My role as a good 2man made me the silent leader of the team without having the pressure and stress of taking the heat if things didn't quite work out.

In 2016, I had the pleasure of co-writing my first book, *It Was All a Dream: If You Can Dream It, You Can Make It Happen. We Did!* I wrote the book with ten of my college buddies who have become successful men in their respective fields. The book served as a fundraiser to help fund our nonprofit organization (www.tdi2r.org) that we established to help provide scholarships, mentoring, and professional development to deserving young college students. Fortunately, I was able to influence these great men to give their money away through this organization and give their story rights over to the organization so we could donate 100 percent of the proceeds of the book to the cause. I don't serve as the president of the group, but I am a founding director and an influencer on the team.

As a management analyst in 1997, I was responsible for overseeing the administrative functions of the Environmental Protection Agency's Houston Laboratory, including the budget, grants, agency processes and procedures, standards for operating procedures, and the representation of our agency through all community outreach efforts. Even though I reported directly to the director, I quickly learned that it was my job to make his job easier and to make him look good.

When I conducted our outreach events, I served on the various cross-governmental agencies' task forces, attended meetings, and came up with creative concepts to make the efforts great. Then when it was time for the big events, I would brief my director on what we had accomplished before he took his seat at the table to accept the awards and the recognitions on behalf of the agency. So it was my job to win victories for him and the agency, and I loved it.

A few years later, I would serve as a 2man to the pastor of my church. He had a vision to start a church from scratch with nothing but an awesome passion for helping people take their lives to the next level and 27 other people, like me, who believed it was possible. My role as a 2 shifted and morphed as the church grew from meeting inside an elementary school to beginning construction on a building sitting on six acres to establishing multiple campuses all over the city.

In one season, I managed the administrative affairs. In another season, I managed the finances before leading the community outreach efforts, managing the staff, and later managing the brand. After more than seven years as a core-team member, I saw a church grow from 29 members to over 7,000. Although my title changed, my role didn't. It was clear that I was a 2man and that my job was to make my #1 look good. I was to interpret his vision and execute it so that he could focus on the things that only he could do, such as preaching, teaching, and casting vision.

Let me clarify who exactly this book is for and what I mean when I talk about 2s. The term *2man* isn't gender-specific, thus it could be a man or a woman. The role you fill and the responsibility you carry is determined by whether you are a 1 or a 2. A 2man is a person in an executive leadership support role whose job it is to add value to the organization, execute the mission, and bring relief to his or her senior leader. In the foreword of Jacquetta Smith's book, *Loyalty: The Pathway to Promotion, Working Up Close and Personal in Ministry*, Dr. I. V. Hillard, Smith's #1, said, "It has been a blessing to have a staff member who can receive your vision, understand your plans, and implement your ideas to the point that it is exactly what you expected."

As you look at some of the most successful organizations in history, you will see that each great leader, or 1, had an influential and brilliant 2. Whether you are a Grace Coddington, who was the secret weapon behind American *Vogue* (the inspiration for the movie *The Devil Wears Prada*); Ed McMahon, Johnny Carson's late-night sidekick who became famous for the line "Heeeeeeeere's Johnny!"; Paul Allen, the less-famous partner of Microsoft; William Henry Seward, President Abraham Lincoln's former presidential-opponent-turned-valuable-cabinet-member and right-hand man; Gayle King, Oprah Winfrey's best friend and editor-at-large for *O Magazine*; Charles Munger, Warren Buffet's right-hand man; a cartoon mouse named Jerry (of *Tom and Jerry*); or Batman's trusted sidekick, Robin—all of these individuals are or were considered 2s who helped their 1s achieve great levels of success and fame.

In the film industry, the 2 is considered the "the right-hand man of The Leader, or second-in-command." This is evident in a sarcastic quote from the character Dr. Evil in the movie *Austin Powers: International Man of Mystery*: "Finally, we come to my number two man. His name . . . Number Two."[1]

Even today in the church sector, there are men and women who serve as amazing 2s to their senior pastors and come alongside them to help strategically execute the 1s' God-given vision. In preparation for writing this book, I have studied and researched some great 2s: Martin E. Hawkins, Billy Hornsby, Jacquetta Smith, Terry Nance, and others who have done a great job writing on this subject. I also interviewed others such as C. C. Hairston (Beacon Light International Baptist Cathedral), Layne Schranz (Highlands Church), Derrick Noble (Full Gospel Baptist Church Fellowship International), Odell Dickerson (New Psalmist Baptist Church), Olus Holder (Fallbrook Church), Drew Corbett (Venue Church), Abram Gomez (Cross Church), Phil Clemens (Faith Church), and Jeff Smith (former assistant to Bishop Michael Pitts and now lead pastor of Strong Tower Church) to get their input on what it takes to be a committed 2, as well as their words of advice to someone new in the position as a 2.

---

[1] tvtropes.org/pmwiki/pmwiki.php/Main/NumberTwo.

CHAPTER TWO
TYPES OF 2S

The first step to being an effective 2man is knowing and understanding your #1, the person as well as his or her vision. Is your #1 a lion like Michael Jordan; or is he an all-around player like Lebron James, looking to get everyone involved, or a distributor, like Jason Kidd? Is your #1 a Moses, diplomatic in style; or is he a Joshua, warrior-like? Is she more like the apostle Paul, straightforward and driven; or is she wishy-washy like Peter? Is he insecure like King Saul or purpose-driven like King David?

Knowing the answers to these questions is important for you to determine what type of leader you're following, because as a 2, your ultimate goal is to complement the 1s, providing help in the areas where they may be weak or covering areas they don't want to cover. If you aren't sure who your leader is and what role he or she will play, or if your leader isn't sure, then you might not be the 2. If you're clear on the direction and your so-called leader isn't, then that may be a sign that you should be driving.

Second, in your role as a 2, 3, 4, or whatever your role may be, you need to know who you are. William Shakespeare said, "To thine own self be true." You will need to find out who you are and what God called and purposed you to do before you can successfully work in your role as a supportive leader. By understanding your unique gift mixes and personality traits, you can better understand how God made you. If you're still trying to explore who you are, complete a spiritual gifts assessment and personality test to help give you better insight.

When I was called to serve my first pastor in 1999, I asked God to help me understand the role I was being called to and to discover what biblical character most related to my role. God took me on a journey that led me to read about Joseph. Once I saw his life—not just when he was the prime minister of Egypt, but his entire life journey—then it resonated with me. He was a dreamer that God turned into an interpreter. I saw character traits, gift mixes, and personalities in him that matched my own. Then I saw his ability to interpret others' dreams and to help make their lives easier.

The name *Joseph* means "to add" or "to bring increase," so I thought I had it. But then God said, "No, study all the Josephs in the Bible." I read about Joseph, Jesus' earthly father. Another Joseph, Joseph of Arimathea, was a rich man who loaned the tomb that Jesus was buried in. The last Joseph in the Bible is Barnabas, the "son of encouragement." He was a generous man who sold his property and laid it at the church leaders' feet so that the mission could continue.

God showed me that there was a common thread running through all of the biblical Josephs. They were willing to come alongside others and give up their gifts and talents to help increase someone else's. They didn't need the spotlight. They were comfortable playing the background and riding in the second chariot. They led from their spot and made a major impact for the kingdom of God.

That was my journey. You may find people in your field who can serve as a compass for your path, but I encourage all Christian leaders to read Scripture and consider the biblical characters to whom they can relate. There are many executive support people in the Bible, including Eve, Joseph (Jacob's son), Aaron, Hur, Joshua, Jonathan, Joab, Nathan, Deborah, Daniel, John the Baptist, Peter, Barnabas, Timothy, and Priscilla and Aquila, just to name a few.

As I was preparing to write this book, I searched the Bible and identified key 2s and executive support staff persons, the qualities that made them special, their spiritual gifts, their personality traits, and the type of 2men they were. The profile of key 2s developed from my research is available for free at www.2mansupport.com, but I encourage you to take time to study these persons and discover which characters you most closely relate to. Understanding these biblical characters has helped me to relate to them and have some form of identity in how God wanted to use me to help my #1.

In his book *Consiglieri: Leading From the Shadows*, Dr. Richard Hytner says there are various roles that a 2man (or a "C," as he calls it) plays: Lodestones, Educators, Anchors, and Deliverers. I conceptually agree with these categories and the outcomes that these roles define. Hytner also says, "There are four feelings that we should make our leader feel: liberated (Lodestones), enlightened (Educators), authentic (Anchors), and decisive (Deliverers)."[1]

For the sake of this book, I am going to use a similar concept but change the names of these roles to Armor-Bearer, Consultant, Friend, and Executioner. I am also going to add the roles of Interpreter, Partner, and Successor. As a 2, you may find that you cross over into more than one of these roles as the need arises. But for the most part, 2men bend in one of these directions as a default to their gift mix or dependent on the type of 1s they work with and what the circumstances were at the time they assumed the role.

Armor-Bearer

The Armor-Bearer is one who brings relief and lightens the load for his or her #1. Terry Nance's book *God's Armor Bearer: Serving God's Leaders* is the best resource ever written on this role. I would do this role an injustice in trying to describe it when he has done such a marvelous job, so I recommend that you stop reading now and order his book.

When most people hear the term *armor-bearer*, they think of the person at church carrying their pastor's Bible and driving him around. Or they think of a personal assistant in the corporate world who serves as an administrative assistant but who doubles as a nanny or a house-sitter as well. Because the focus of this book is on 2men executives, I am not referring to those roles, even though a 2man may do all of that at times. Instead, my focus on the role of Armor-Bearer is on how he or she brings relief or lightens the load for a 1.

An Armor-Bearer looks at the projects the 1 has and asks to handle some of them so the leader can focus on the things that only leaders can do. Armor-Bearers say, "I can handle that meeting for you. I will make that call. Let me deal with that unproductive staff member or disrespectful client."

Chapter Two

Consultant

The Consultant is one who advises a leader on decisions. Discussion of this role is the essence of Richard Hytner's book *Consiglieri: Leading From the Shadows*. When most people think of the term *consigliere* (singular), they think of the term made popular in the movie trilogy *The Godfather*. In the mafia, the consigliere, or "counselor," is the man who advises the mob boss, sits in on meetings, and negotiates deals on the boss's behalf. The consigliere is not considered a threat to the boss's position because he serves to gain his boss's best interests through his role as chancellor or counselor.

In the same way, a Consultant is not a yes-man but is often the only person who is able to challenge a leader's decisions and play devil's advocate to make sure the best decisions are made for the organization. This role can be seen in the biblical personalities of Priscilla and Aquila. They brought pastors into their home and served as consultants to advise them on how to properly handle the Word of God. The Christian preacher Apollos and the apostle Paul were a few of those who benefited from their work.

Friend

The Friend is the 2man who serves as a trusted confidant and friend. One of the clearest illustrations of a Friend can be found in the relationship between the biblical Jonathan and David. Jonathan was the son of King Saul and heir apparent to the throne by birth. Although he was next in line to become a 1, he befriended a young man named David, who at the time served as an armor-bearer to the king.

We see a few qualities in Jonathan's relationship with David that may apply to the role of a 2. First, Jonathan looked out for his #1 despite the odds. He was willing to spare his own job security in order to secure David's well-being. Second, David could confide in his #2 about anything and trust that his secrets would go to the grave. Third, Jonathan loved David as if he were his own flesh and blood. Finally, Jonathan made his friend's success his top priority, even at the risk of not being as successful himself.

Executioner

Of all the roles I'm listing in this book, I identify most closely with that of Executioner, and I think that all the leaders under whom I have served would agree. I learned my role from trial and error and much practice, and I honestly believe God anointed me for it.

An Executioner's job is to execute strategies developed by the 1, and he or she typically takes responsibility for delivering results on a day-to-day basis. As an Executioner, I like to describe my role in two ways: I execute the vision of my leader, and I execute all resistance to that vision. Like Hytner's "Deliverer," I know when to set the ambiance in the room so my leader can feed off my energy and thrive. I know when to be a fixer who is not concerned about how others feel but who is there to lay the hatchet down and remove the bodies that stand in resistance.

On many occasions, I am the one responsible for delivering the bad news or firing employees. (I'm sorry. *Repositioning of purpose transactions* is the more politically-correct term.) I may need prayer because I believe I may have gotten too good in this area. When your wife nicknames you "Iron Hand" and other organizations are contracting you to come and reposition their staff, then you may need to go and sit on someone's couch for a conversation.

The role of Executioner is not an easy one to play because you become the "leader they love to hate," and it doesn't come with much fanfare. So if you are one who feeds off the good opinions of others and wants to be liked by everyone on your team above your leader's vision, then I would ask you to question if you are called to be a 2man. Because no matter which type you are, at some point, you may have to play the role of Executioner.

Interpreter

An Interpreter is one who explains or presents something in understandable terms or one who brings to realization by demonstration. Interpreters translate the visionary's plan, makes it plain, and then executes it to perfection. Visionaries need help interpreting their visions and communicating them effectively with employees, congregations, vendors, and community partners. So Interpreters are strategists and organizational architects who work alongside their leaders to help develop systems and plans in order to bring their visions to pass.

Good biblical examples of Interpreters are Joseph and Daniel. These men were able to hear the visions that their leaders had, tell them what they meant, and then tell them what they should do with those visions. God gave them a unique gifting and anointing that allowed them to serve as essential secret weapons for their #1s. Joseph's ability allowed him to rise in power and become the second-in-command in Egypt—or as some have called him, the prime minister of Egypt. Daniel served in the capacity of a 2 so well that he served multiple kings.

Along with my role as an Executioner, I equally serve in the capacity of Interpreter with my pastor; and my skills in this role are the basis of the company I founded, BNB Consulting & Associates. The focus of BNB is to help visionaries identify, interpret, and strategically transform their visions into realities.

Partner

In some sense, all 2s partner with their 1s to help bring the vision to pass for the organization, but there are some people who may serve more as a Partner than any other role. They share the same level of responsibility for the success of the organization, may have started the organization with the 1s, and/or are an irreplaceable component of the organization. There aren't many people who serve in this capacity alone, but they do exist.

In the corporate world, a company may bring in a 2 not as a mentor but as a foil to complement the CEO's experience, style, knowledge base, or penchants. Observers have viewed the relationships between Bill Gates and two of his previous COOs, Jon Shirley and Michael Hallman, in this light. Other people such as Paul Allen (Bill Gates, Microsoft), Steve Wozniak (Steve Jobs, Apple), Rushion McDonald (Steve Harvey, *The Steve Harvey Show*), Rick Rubin (Russell Simmons, Def Jam), and famous entertainer Dean Martin (Jerry Lewis) would have been considered Partners.

I have identified biblical persons who could be considered 2men but who were also Partners. Eve and Aaron are two of these unique individuals. Eve was Adam's wife, but Adam couldn't have carried out his assignment without her. She was the suitable helper he needed to give birth to the rest of mankind. Her partnership role showed up in the Creation story; and she held an influential voice in their partnership, one that led to them ultimately being terminated from their assignment for insubordination.

Aaron served as Moses' 2man in helping emancipate the children of Israel from Egyptian slavery. Although he didn't have the same pressure as Moses, who was the clear leader, Aaron was a vital partner in God's plan for his people.

If you are a Partner, be careful because similar to the Successor, ambition can derail your relationship with your leader. There is a reason people attribute one partner as the 1 and not the other, despite the partnership. The quicker you realize this and are OK with it, the sooner you and your leader can move forward, play your roles, and achieve success. The first woman in the world, Eve, desired to be like The Ultimate #1, God, and see how quickly that got her kicked out of the company headquarters!

Successor

Successors are those who serve as 2s for a period of time but who will eventually succeed their 1s and become a 1 in their own right. Some Successors come into this position with the goal of eventually becoming a 1, and they use this position as a stepping stone to that role. Others may become a Successor without even seeking the position, but they serve faithfully in their 2man role. Martin E. Hawkins calls these people reluctant 2s. They possess all the necessary qualities of a 2, such as humility, loyalty, and excellence; and when their leaders are ready to transition, they can't think of anyone else who would be more qualified to replace them, so the Successor becomes the leader.

Jeff Smith served as an assistant to Bishop Michael Pitts, founding pastor of Cornerstone Church. Smith says, "[Serving as a 2man] gave me the opportunity to see and participate in ministry from three different vantage points. After serving in various roles, areas, and projects, I developed a capacity and an affinity to help churches and pastors with leadership development, strategic planning, and systems implementation." He now serves as lead pastor of Strong Tower, but he still serves Bishop Pitts and oversees Cornerstone Global Network.

In Scripture, there are many people who started out serving in one role and then later were promoted to the #1 spot. You read about reluctant successors such as Joshua and Elisha. These men had no clue that they were being prepared for that spot and had no desire to be the leading character. One could assume that if it weren't for a mistake or a failure of their leaders, they may never have been selected for the leadership role.

Joshua was promoted because Moses disobeyed God's command. Elisha was minding his own business, tending to cattle before Elijah had a mental meltdown on Mount Horeb and was ready to take his life. God spoke to Elijah about Elisha and told him to select him because he would one day assume the prophet's role when he was taken off the scene. On the other hand, you have people like David who knew that one day he would be king, but he faithfully served Saul until his time came.

As a 2man, it's important for you to serve in your role with contentment and not to push for the #1-spot. I've seen people who allowed their ambition to cause them to finagle their way to the top spot only to be silenced, exposed, and ultimately fired. And I've seen those who were selected specifically to be a Successor, but they became frustrated or impatient with the process. Instead of continuing to work to be the best 2s they could be, which is what put their names on the map in the first place, they made a mess of things by wanting to skip ahead too soon.

After reading about what a 2man is and the various roles he or she may play, let me leave you with the greatest example. When I think of what it means to be a 2man, I find the greatest example is not Joseph, Barnabas, or any other earthly person. The best example is Jesus Himself.

God is #1 and needed an Executioner to carry out His plans. Philippians 2:6-8 (NIV) says, "Who, being in very nature God, did not consider equality with God something to be used to his own advantage; rather, he made himself nothing by taking the very nature of a servant, being made in human likeness. And being found in appearance as a man, he humbled himself by becoming obedient to death—even death on a cross!" Jesus came down from His Partner role and became an Executioner.

Associate Pastor Martin E. Hawkins said, "Perhaps the best analogy for how the multi-staff should function relationally is the Trinity. The Father gives the order and vision, the Son obeys and serves, and the third chair, the Spirit, humbly makes sure that the work of the other two gets completed. . . . God is not God without the second and third chair."[2]

The hope for the faithful 2man is that, eventually, God will take notice of your service. Despite the fact that you might not receive accolades from your peers and from those you serve, God sees and will elevate you in due time.

---

[1]*Consiglieri: Leading From the Shadows*, by Richard Hytner (Profile Books, 2014); page 192.
[2]*The Associate Pastor: Second Chair, Not Second Best,* by Martin E. Hawkins with Kelli Sallman (B&H Books, 2005); pages 11-12.

CHAPTER THREE
THE QUALITIES OF A 2: PART 1

n writing this chapter, I took time to think about my journey and some of the key qualities that I feel a 2man must have, based on my experience. As you will notice in the 2man profile located on www.2mansupport.com, a 2 should be **H**umble, **H**ealthy, **O**bedient, **O**rganized, **R**esourceful, **R**esilient, **S**ubmitted, **S**trategic, **E**xcellent, and an **E**xample. These qualities make up what I call the H.O.R.S.E. for your #1 and your organization. I use horses for this illustration as a metaphor and as an acronym because horses are creatures that evolve with the times. Here are some key facts about horses.[1]

- The anatomy of horses enables them to use speed to escape predators and gives them a well-developed sense of balance and a strong fight-or-flight response.
- Related to their need to flee from predators in the wild, horses are able to sleep standing up or lying down.
- Horses have the largest eyes of any land mammal; and they are lateral-eyed, meaning that their eyes are positioned on the sides of their heads. Therefore, horses have a range of vision of more than 350 degrees.
- Horses' sense of smell, while much better than that of humans, is not quite as good as that of dogs. It is believed to play a key role in horses' social interactions as well as in detecting other key scents in their environment.
- A horse's hearing is good, and the pinna of each ear can rotate up to 180 degrees, giving the potential for 360-degree hearing without having to move its head.
- Horses are able to sense contact as subtle as an insect landing anywhere on their bodies.

- Total sleep time in a 24-hour period may range from several minutes to a couple of hours, mostly in short intervals of about 15 minutes each.
- Communication between human and horse is paramount in any equestrian activity. A horse is usually ridden with a saddle on its back, to assist the rider with balance and positioning, and a bridle or related headgear, to assist the rider in maintaining control.

The Lion and the Horse Revelation

One day, I had a discovery while talking to my #1. He was challenging our executive team to be lions, leaders, and aggressive go-getters. I understood exactly where he was coming from, because to run the type of organization we run requires tough, strategic, purpose-driven people with entrepreneurial spirits.

I considered myself to be one of the lion pack until I started doing research on horses. My #1 is a lion and needs to be in order to continue to lead us to success and execute the many goals we have. But as his #2, I need to be a horse for him and for the organization. Horses represent stability, can sense when things are changing, and are sensitive to when danger is approaching. Whereas lions are wild, horses can be domesticated for the greater good, which means they are built for others to ride on them without breaking down. Lions drag things, but horses are built to carry.

Seeing the difference between lions and horses was an important revelation for me. It helped me to understand that a great 2man exhibits all the qualities of a horse, from the speed in which we accomplish tasks to our wide range of vision to see the big picture to our great sense of balance to allow us to multitask well to the ability to grind for long periods of time without much sleep. Successful 2s also understand the benefit of being willing to be saddled, which helps our #1s remain balanced so they can get to their destination, as well as taking on the bridle, which in our job is necessary to guard our mouths so we can keep matters confidential at all times.

I can assure you that your organization needs you to be more horse-like than lion-like. Let your #1 roar you to victory while you successfully carry the daily loads.

So how can you take on more of a horse's best qualities so you can serve your lion more effectively? Consider the following attributes that make up a H.O.R.S.E.

H: Humble and Healthy

Humility is the top quality in being a great 2man. Humility is a state of selflessness that requires you to put others' needs before your own without expecting to receive credit and applause for your accomplishments. I learned humility when I made mistakes and was corrected publicly, such as when I spoke ahead of my leader and was wrong or when I bragged about what I did to help the company, thus taking victories away from my leader.

My first pastor used to pray, "Lord, teach me humility before you have to humble me." Fortunately, I learned these lessons early in the game because if I hadn't I wouldn't be writing this book today. Humility has helped me understand that it is not important if I'm credited for my plans, creative ideas, or the concepts that were a huge win for the organization. As long as my leader implemented them and they worked for us, then together we won.

The people give the credit to the leader, and that is who deserves it. He was the one smart enough to hire me, wise enough to see I had a good plan, and courageous enough to implement it. If it didn't work and he ran with it, then I wouldn't expect him to come across the pulpit and tell the people that we tried the plan and it didn't work, so blame Ramone Harper. All the risk is with the leader, so if he gets the credit and the applause, so be it. My number one goal is to help him win victories organizationally and personally and to help our vision for the movement come to pass.

Being *Healthy* is another prerequisite for mastering humility. Only healthy and emotionally secure people can be humble. For as long as I have served as a 2man, I have constantly had to work on my personal health in order to remain effective. Health, in this context, refers to all categories of health such as physical, emotional, relational, financial, and mental.

Pastor Dharius Daniels, senior leader of Change Church, often says it's easier to catch sickness than it is to catch health. Being healthy requires work, discipline, and commitment over the long haul. In our roles as 2men, the healthier we are, the greater longevity we can have. For better physical health, we must exercise and eat healthy. If we don't take care of our bodies, then we won't be helpful to anyone long-term. To improve emotionally, deal with the stones in your heart that may have developed from unmet needs from your past and take time to properly grieve the losses you have experienced.

In relationships, set proper boundaries with family, friends, co-workers, and church members. Learn the power of forgiveness. You *will* be offended on numerous occasions, and you can't successfully help your #1 if you hold grudges and don't let things roll off of you. Solid financial health is imperative as you will be spending long hours in your role as a 2, and money is one thing that you don't want to worry about. From creating and managing your budget, to living within your means, to saving and investing for a rainy day and emergencies, being financially healthy is critical.

And don't neglect your mental health. My wife is a licensed therapist, and she often asks her clients, "How is your mental health?" One out of five people suffer from mental illness in many forms, including depression, schizophrenia, grief, and bipolarism. At Change Church, we strongly encourage members to seek counseling in conjunction with prayer as part of the healing process. Pastor Daniels preached a message called "What Are You Doing Here?" when speaking of another well-known 2. He asked, "Are you healthy enough to be a John the Baptist?"

O: Obedient and Organized

Obedient 2men do the tasks assigned and get them done quickly and efficiently. But they're not obedient just so they can check items off their never-ending to-do lists. One day, Pastor Daniels told our staff that the timeliness in which we accomplish the assignments he gives us builds trust. If he has to work around us to get things done, that isn't a good sign.

Obedience is showcased in the biblical story of Abraham's servant who was sent to find a wife for Abraham's son Isaac (Genesis 24). Abraham was on his dying bed and wanted a wife for his son from among his own family. Not only did his servant obey his leader's instructions, but he did it immediately and exactly as he was instructed.

As a horse, you must be obedient and willing to be led. In his book *How to Lead When You're Not in Charge: Leveraging Influence When You Lack Authority,* Clay Scroggins says you have to do two things to master obedience: First, lead yourself. Second, model followership. In other words, every great leader is following someone or something.[2] Can you follow the leader you're working for? If not, you might as well stop reading now.

Have you ever seen a racehorse buck its rider? What was the outcome? I guarantee you 100 out of 100 times that when a horse decides to stop obeying its rider that the pair loses the race and disaster happens, not only causing injury to the horse and its rider but to others on the track, too.

In her book *Loyalty: The Pathway to Promotion, Working Up Close and Personal in Ministry,* Jacquetta Smith encourages us to "get organized by getting an organizer or planner."[3] Nowadays, being **Organized** isn't difficult. You can have all of your organizational tools right on your phone or tablet.

It's important for a 2man to be able to write goals and execute them with precision. Next to the Bible, your most important tool is a calendar. You have to be able to use a calendar strategically to help you accomplish tasks and manage projects on a yearly, quarterly, monthly, weekly, and daily basis. The projects and assignments you will work on will vary, so you must be able to organize yourself in such a way that will help you be most effective.

You don't have to use the same tools as everyone else. Search the internet or your local bookstore or office supply store for the tools that best fit your personality, working style, and project needs.

You can be as technologically advanced as Wunderlist or Zoho project management software or as old-school as a Franklin Covey planner. I teach a method called "The Interpretation Process" that is a quality practical tool to help support staff work in excellence with their leaders in carrying out projects. But whatever methods you use, make sure they work best for you.

R: Resourceful and Resilient

Being **Resourceful** can set you apart as a 2man. When your leader can come to you with a new project and you are able to leverage your relationships and networks in order to get the job done faster than anyone else, then you continue to make yourself valuable to your organization. For example, having relationships with vendors who are willing to give you the best deal possible or being able to reach out to bankers, community leaders, and government officials to help move your project faster helps you to be an invaluable resource to your #1.

In *Success for the Second in Command: Leading From the Second Chariot*, Billy Hornsby writes, "When you are able to connect and partner with great leaders and their causes, you gain influence from them that helps you fulfill greater goals than ever before. . . . It is my conviction that you should do everything in your power to leverage the influence of the organization you work for and the influence of your leader. This promotes what they are doing, and in return you get . . . *influence*."[4]

Resilience is the capacity to recover quickly from difficulties or the ability to spring back into shape, requiring toughness and elasticity. It's essential to have tough skin in this business and not wear your emotions on your sleeve. Ministry and business are not for the weak of heart. At times, you will make mistakes, and you will be disappointed and hurt. But resilience is the ability to bounce back.

Good 2men should always remain flexible so that if they are stretched, they will be able to snap back into place. If you don't have this quality, pray for it, tarry for it. If you don't, then get out of this role quickly!

S: Submitted and Strategic

Recently, Pastor Daniels wrote a book called *RePresent Jesus: Rethink Your Christianity and Become More Like Christ*, and in it he describes what he calls the "S-word." Often, people try to avoid the word *submission* because they associate it with weakness. Pastor Daniels wrote, "The term *submission* has been historically mishandled, theologically misused, and often taken out of biblical context—but just because it has been abused does not mean it should be avoided."[5]

Pastor Daniels defines *submission* as a combination of two root words: *sub* and *mission*. He says that the overall goal of submission is to get under the mission. Jesus is the best example of someone who submitted Himself to God's plan for humanity (Philippians 2). As a 2man, follow His example, and be willing to be **Submitted** to God's purpose for your life and to your leader in order to be successful.

In the roles we play as executive leadership support, we must be **Strategic** in our thinking and in our time management. Joseph is a primary example of a strategic thinker. After he interpreted Pharaoh's vision of abundance and imminent lack, he formulated a strategic plan on how to manage Egypt's resources.

> "And now let Pharaoh look for a discerning and wise man and put him in charge of the land of Egypt. Let Pharaoh appoint commissioners over the land to take a fifth of the harvest of Egypt during the seven years of abundance. They should collect all the food of these good years that are coming and store up the grain under the authority of Pharaoh, to be kept in the cities for food. This food should be held in reserve for the country, to be used during the seven years of famine that will come upon Egypt, so that the country may not be ruined by the famine. The plan seemed good to Pharaoh and to all his officials. So Pharaoh asked them, 'Can we find anyone like this man, one in whom is the spirit of God?' " (Genesis 41:33-38).

Joseph used Pharaoh's vision to form a strategy and manage its implementation to save the lives of millions of people during a famine. Effective 2men have to employ their strategic skill sets in assisting their #1s to interpret their visions and transform them into reality.

E: Excellent and Example

While serving as a consultant for Dr. Timothy W. Sloan, pastor of The Luke Church in Humble, Texas, I learned the slogan he uses to help his leadership staff understand their team philosophy: "Efficiency + Effectiveness = *Excellence*."

To be efficient means working in an organized way and achieving maximum productivity with minimum wasted effort and expenses. If you oversee operations or finances, then efficiency is everything for you. The more efficient you are, the more time and money you save the organization.

To be effective, on the other hand, is successfully achieving a desired goal or objective. This is the equivalent of Joseph's work in Egypt.

"The LORD was with Joseph so that he prospered, and he lived in the house of his Egyptian master. When his master saw that the LORD was with him and that the LORD gave him success in everything he did, Joseph found favor in his eyes and became his attendant. Potiphar put him in charge of his household, and he entrusted to his care everything he owned" (Genesis 39:2-4).

The combination of efficiency and effectiveness develops your spirit of excellence. But excellence is much more than what you do and more of the way you think. Excellence is ninety percent mental and only ten percent mechanical. One of the key philosophies of my company is that excellence would be the standard, not the goal. Make it your top priority to please God and to be excellent in everything you do. If you please God, then you will blow your #1's mind.

Of all of these H.O.R.S.E. qualities, being an *Example* is perhaps the best leadership quality and one of the greatest assets a 2man can bring to the organization. Your leader needs someone to point to who embodies the culture traits, the core values, the change that the vision requires, and the excellence that they want others to operate in. In most cases, your example will speak louder than your words.

Allow your #1, the lion, to roar and cast vision; but as the horse, you can then exemplify the vision. The people in your organization or your clientele need to see what the #1 has been saying through someone other than the senior leader. As a horse, you stabilize the organization by showing up and not saying a word. Just be what the leader says.

For example, if your leader says that showing up on time for a meeting makes everyone late, then as a 2, you should be sitting in the conference room 15 minutes before the meeting begins with computer up, pen and notepad ready, and cell phone off. If the 1 wants everyone to be responsive to customers' emails or phone calls because responsiveness shows people that you honor them, then never be the one people are complaining about. Not only do 2s operate in excellence, but they also are examples of what the 1s' visions look like lived out loud.[6]

---

[1]Adapted from the Wikipedia article "Horse" (en.wikipedia.org/wiki/Horse).

[2]How to Lead When You're Not in Charge: Leveraging Influence When You Lack Authority, by Clay Scroggins (Zondervan, 2017); page 96.

[3]Loyalty: The Pathway to Promotion, Working Up Close and Personal in Ministry, by Jacquetta Brown Smith (VJS Productions, Inc., 2003).

[4]Success for the Second in Command: Leading From the Second Chariot, by Billy Hornsby (Creation House, 2005); page 35.

[5]RePresent Jesus: Rethink Your Version of Christianity and Become More Like Christ, by Dharius Daniels (Charisma House, 2014); page 67.

[6]R.I.P. to my friend A. L. Patterson who encouraged the world to LOL, live out loud!

CHAPTER FOUR
THE QUALITIES OF A 2: PART 2

n my interviews with current 2men (for which I am extremely grateful because they took time out of their busy schedules to assist me in this effort), I found their answers to be exhaustive but necessary to consider. While I agree with all of my interviewees' responses, there is one person who gave such a unique spin on my questions that I had to expound upon it.

Layne Schranz serves as associate pastor under Pastor Chris Hodges at Church of the Highlands in Alabama. He has served for over 28 years, with more than 16 years in his current capacity. Church of the Highlands doesn't have a traditional 2man-structure because it operates with a leadership team of nine executives, but I still see Layne as a good example of a 2man.

Layne teaches that the top quality a 2man must possess is to be a son or daughter of the house, and he teaches how to be an heir. He attributes this mindset to his success and longevity in the role. I pray that he writes a book on the topic, which is desperately needed in the religious world.

In addition to the qualities that my counterparts listed and those I shared in Chapter 3, there are two more that I feel are so quintessential and closely related that they need their own chapter. If grace and mercy are spiritual twins, then in the 2man role, confidentiality and loyalty are success twins.

Confidentiality

As a 2man, more than likely you will serve as chief of staff or leader of leaders, which means you will be privy to sensitive information. Your leader will share things with you in confidence that you can never repeat to anyone.

Many times, you will see your leader at his most vulnerable and human state, and you will need to keep him covered. You may be exposed to your leader's flaws and weaknesses and need to help her through it. When you hear about plans and visions before anyone else, you won't be able to share them until your leader is ready to share. You will also find yourself in the company of other leaders who need to feel safe with you around, and you will probably be privy to their personal and confidential conversations because you are in the room.

You shouldn't share any of this information with the rest of the staff, the congregation, or your spouse. In ministry there are things you will need to withhold from your spouse because if you expose that information, it could be detrimental to your role, to the vision of the church, and to the success of the ministry.

Your leader depends on you to be discreet and keep certain information confidential. If you are hurt, disappointed, or offended, or if you feel the need to vent or to share confidential information with your spouse, it may come back to haunt you. Your breach of confidentiality could destroy your spouse's spiritual development because he or she is part of the congregation, too. You can't confide in other staff members either because you are responsible for leading them. And if you get the reputation of someone who repeats secrets, then you might as well pack your bags.

Confidentiality is also a major key to loyalty. The story of Noah's sons is a prime biblical example. Noah, who at the time was the savior of the world because of his obedience to God in building the ark, got drunk on his own success, as my pastor likes to say, after he drank wine from a vineyard he had planted. One of his sons, Ham, saw him inebriated and told his two brothers, Shem and Japheth, about it. Ham had exposed his father's (leader's) nakedness to his brothers.

When Shem and Japheth heard what had happened to Noah, they did the right thing. First, they rebuked Ham for mocking their father while Noah was in such a state. Then they took a sheet and walked backward into the tent so they wouldn't see Noah's nakedness while they covered him up, and they never talked of the incident again.

Because Ham exposed his father's nakedness, his seed was cursed. What a scary thought! Because of Ham's wickedness in uncovering his leader, not only was he demoted in the family business, but what he would give birth to would be cursed and would suffer the consequences of his actions.

This is the same principal I have seen played out in my almost 20 years in ministry. Some people talk about their leaders or expose their weaknesses to others and think they are doing a good deed or are getting revenge. At the time, it may not seem as if they are suffering any consequences. But over time, they are never able to produce anything worth mentioning or are never able to be productive in anything else. If they leave the church and try to start their own, it flops. If they try to start a business, it flops. Their lack of confidentiality even affects their family lives. Many of them experience divorce, severe illnesses, or worse.

Make sure you can see and hear confidential information but still be able to serve. As a 2man, you should make it your business to see no evil; hear no evil; and, more importantly, speak no evil. Bottom line, to be successful as a 2man, keep your mouth shut!

Loyalty

"Loyalty is tested by how you respond to offense and how you respond to opportunities." Brian Houston, senior pastor of Hillsong Church in Sydney, New South Wales, Australia, shared this statement with my pastor, Dr. Dharius Daniels, and other leaders while they were in New Zealand.

Many times, I have been offended, whether it was being embarrassed in front of the rest of the staff by the leader, moving forward with a plan that was agreed upon only to find out by someone else that my leader had changed his mind and I was the last to know, or not being in the loop about important changes or shifts in the organization. But despite how I felt or how offended I was, I had to remember that God called me to my position. Each time, I had to pray for wisdom on how to handle the situation.

Sometimes God led me to swallow my pride and get over it. As the leader of the church, the pastor has the right to do whatever he feels is best for the organization, and that may not have included checking in with me first. Other times, God led me to be patient and wait for Him to create an opportunity for me and my leader to discuss the situation. This always seems to work well because sure enough something would happen or come up that would create a chance for me to speak plainly and truthfully in love about how I felt. Sometimes the situation resulted from an honest misunderstanding, and my leader didn't know I was offended, or he would hear my heart and apologize.

Your experiences may differ from mine. But no matter what situation you experience, the best thing to do is to go to God in prayer and wait for Him to lead you.

As a 2man, I have been presented with many opportunities. While serving as COO at my first church, our ministry began to experience fast and supernatural growth in a short amount of time. Pastors from all over the country were inquiring about what we were doing, what strategies we were using to reach people and brand the ministry, and how we were finding and developing our staff. Many times, my pastor would tell them to talk with me because I managed the day-to-day operations. This opportunity led to me consulting with many pastors and members of their staffs, and one of the most common things they said to me was, "I wish we had a person like you on our staff. It would make life so much easier."

Because of my 2man skill set, I was offered opportunities to leave that ministry. But I wanted to be loyal to my leader, so I decided to consult only with those pastors he referred to me or who he asked me to help. This was my way of being loyal to my leader, and it worked in my favor and caused other pastors to appreciate me and what I was doing.

Loyalty is a serious issue, and you have to be clear on what God is calling you to do and to whom He is calling you to serve because sometimes the lines get blurry. During that season, it was important for me to focus my energy and time on what we were trying to accomplish with the vision God gave my pastor, and I had to remember that I wouldn't even have had those opportunities if it weren't for him.

Once, I was presented with an out-of-this-world opportunity to accept a position with a ministry in my hometown that was four to five times the size of my current ministry. They were willing to make me an offer that most people wouldn't refuse. I was told to name my asking price and it would be done. The offer was amazing, and it was a great opportunity to be part of something bigger; but I was already committed to something great and someone great. I was clear that God had called me to my pastor and to the work that we were doing to change as many lives as possible for God's glory and for their good.

I respectfully declined the offer immediately and offered to help them find the right person. Afterward, I told my wife and my pastor about it. Although, I knew the offer was great, I also realized that it was a test of my loyalty.

In *Shoulder to Shoulder: Strengthening Your Church by Support-ing Your Pastor*, Dan Reiland makes a point that perfectly supports my thoughts on loyalty: "While we know that our ultimate first loyalty is to God, every church leader must settle this question: Is my loyalty first to the mission of the church or to the pastor? The question is difficult and opens much debate, but the answer must be, 'To the Pastor.' Leaders in the church must first be loyal to the pastor, then to the mission, because the pastor is assumed to be loyal to the mission. If that is true, your loyalty will be transferred directly into the mission. It doesn't work the other way around."[1]

Reiland's point is true, but it is also biblical. When Jesus called his disciples, He called them to be with Him first and the mission second: "Follow me, and I will make you fishers of men" (Matthew 4:19, KJV).

---

[1]*Shoulder to Shoulder: Strengthening Your Church by Supporting Your Pastor*, by Dan Reiland (Thomas Nelson, 1997); page 169.

THE MOTIVATIONS OF A 2

otivation is the reason for a person's actions or desires, and sometimes it can be a two-edged sword. Motivation often drives people's behaviors, good and bad. So although a person is motivated, that doesn't mean his or her actions will result in good consequences.

The first question I ask people who serve in executive leadership support roles and want me to mentor them is, "Why are you in this?" It's important for me to know what they're hoping to gain by serving in this capacity. If their response includes the phrases "It's a stepping stone to my next level," "It will give me time to put my own thing together," "It's the only role available," "It pays the bills," or anything similar, the red lights, my horse ears, and my sixth sense go into full steam. Immediately, I recommend that they get out of the 2man role. I advise them to schedule a meeting with their direct supervisors and begin the dreaded transition conversation.

On the flip side, there is such a thing as positive motivation, and I heartily encourage it. I co-authored a book with ten of my partners from the nonprofit organization Turning Dreams Into Realities (www.tdi2r.org), which focuses on providing mentorship, scholarships, and professional development to young people. In our book, *It Was All a Dream*, we share that one of the keys to making dreams come true is motivation or self-motivation.

One person we reference in the supplementary *It Was All a Dream* workbook is DJ Khaled, an entertainer and social media superstar who writes motivational Snapchats and Instagram posts. If you aren't following him @djkhaled, then you are missing out. He is the ultimate self-motivator, and he inspires the world with his "Major Keys to Success" with such motivational nuggets as "They don't want you to win," "Be a star. Be a superstar," "I remember when I ain't have no Jacuzzi," and "All I do is win, win, win no matter what."

Wrong Motivations

In Chapter Three, I list one of the key qualities of a successful 2man as health. Serving in an executive leadership support role in any organization requires you to be healthy in every aspect of your life. You will experience many diverse negative situations such as peer pressure, lack of recognition, lack of appreciation, lack of exposure, disrespect from team members and family, feelings of not being enough, anxiety, and stress—just to name a few. So good health and pure motives must be in your toolkit.

American psychologist Abraham Maslow defined the hierarchy of needs that influence our behaviors as basic human needs. These include the need for food and water, shelter and safety, social acceptance, recognition and self-esteem, and self-actualization. He also said that only unsatisfied needs influence behavior; satisfied needs do not. So if you are motivated to be in the 2man role or are pondering getting into this position for any of these reasons, then don't!

My wife likes to say, "Life is rude," and during a particular season in my life, I had to amen her. Early in 2016, I called my pastor and told him that I felt as if I were hitting a wall and needed to see somebody. It just felt like the world was weighing down on me, and I felt as if I were being suffocated. In the past few years, I had experienced loss of loved ones (my father to cancer and my granddaughter to SIDS); I had made major relocation moves that separated me from my wife and children for extended periods of time; I had given up my business and closed it for a second time to serve in my current capacity; and the list goes on and on.

My pastor recommended that I immediately go to a healing heart retreat in North Carolina that had helped him through his own experiences. While at this retreat in the middle of "Nowhere," North Carolina, this little lady and her husband spoke to me about stony hearts and unmet needs. Faster than you can download the newest app to your phone, I felt my walls coming down and going into my sunken place. The couple helped me see that I had built up walls around my heart as a protective mechanism because of unmet needs that I had had as a child. Thanks to that time away and that wise, loving couple, I'm in a better place today.

I have seen many unhealthy people in leadership positions, including spiritual leaders. The 2man role is not a role you take on in order to address your unmet needs of affirmation, security, or esteem. But, unfortunately, many people do it for just that reason. Thus, they end up frustrated, upset, and downright angry and ready to blame the company for their disappointment. Church leaders can fall into this sunken place so hard that they leave their posts, leave their churches, and leave God altogether. What was the problem? Their motivations were in the wrong place.

Right Motivations

My list of right motivations for serving as a 2man is short and simple: (A) You're called to it, (B) you have a love for the leader who needs your support, (C) you have a love and a passion for seeing the vision of that organization come to pass, or (D) a combination of any of the above. I would go so far as to say that it should be A, B, and C; but sometimes you can start with one and grow into the others.

Called. For those in the church sphere, our understanding of a calling is something that God Himself speaks to us through His Word, a prophetic voice, or some sort of divinely inspired vision that He gives us that makes it super clear that this is what we should be doing with our lives. For those who don't subscribe to the religious jargon that we Christians profess, I still believe you should feel a sense of calling and purpose to the jobs you do.

Steve Jobs and Bill Gates were called to start and develop the way people connect with others via technology. Others discovered their skills and gifts to use their hands in ways that most people can't comprehend, whether it was to fix cars, style hair, bake desserts, program computers, or whatever it is. When you're called, you just know it, and you have to attribute it to a higher power greater than yourself. Have you ever wondered why you know something or know how to handle certain things instinctively without ever learning about it before? That's a calling, and you have to pay attention to that.

Love for the leader. The second motivation is the love for your leader and your desire to see him or her win. This is a dedication and a devotion to want to see your leader win in ways that the normal person doesn't. For some reason, when you hear your leader speak, hear who she is, and what she is trying to accomplish, you feel as if you were born to help her in whatever she does.

When I felt called to serve my first pastor, I was working with the children's ministry teaching third-graders and part of our young adult ministry. One Sunday, I heard our senior pastor say that our young adult pastor would be leaving the church to organize his own church. Even though I was a student of this young man's teaching, I didn't know him personally.

Late one night after teaching my class, I packed up and headed home. Something (well, I know what and Who it was) made me get halfway down the Beltway home and turn around and go back to the church. Guess who was the only one left at the church, closing it down for the first time ever? My young adult pastor. That night, we sat and talked for hours about who he was, what he felt God was calling him to do, and how he wanted to help people go to the next level in their lives; and something just clicked. I told him I would be praying for him and talking to my wife about it. Actually, I didn't need to hear anything else because I knew I was supposed to help him in whatever capacity he needed me. My motivation was to help him and see him win.

A few months later, we were starting Higher Dimension Church at his father's house, with 29 members. My little apartment became our first office and administrative headquarters. Soon after, we held our first worship service in a school, with 500 people in attendance and hundreds joining that day. In a few years, with me serving as deacon and COO, we had grown from 29 members to thousands. I didn't know what the outcome would be and, to tell the truth, I didn't care. I just knew that I loved him and that I was supposed to help him in that season.

Passion for the vision. The last motivation should be a passion for the vision. Steve Jobs said, "If you are working on something that you really care about, you don't have to be pushed. The vision pulls you." The leader of your organization shouldn't be the only one who can't sleep at night because ideas and strategies are coming to her in dreams. When a real 2man hears the vision, he or she goes into what I call "The Interpretation Process." The vision for the company becomes your vision, and the desire to see it become a reality becomes your obsession.

Discussing the interpretation process reminds me of the biblical Joseph, who at one stage in his life had his own dreams of success. Through various trials and tribulations, his vision became to help others' visions come to pass. When he heard someone's dream, he would interpret that vision and make it plain for his leader. Joseph eventually became the prime minister of Egypt because not only was he able to interpret the dreams of his #1 and put them into practical strategies, but he was also able to manage the dream in a way to make it come to pass and increase the profits of his organization like none other.

I have learned in my role as 2man that some people have the ability to dream and see visions but that it takes another one, an interpreter, to come along and translate that dream into a strategic plan. People like Steve Stoute, author of *The Tanning of America: How Hip-Hop Created a Culture That Rewrote the Rules of the New Economy* and founder of the brand development and marketing firm Translation, has that gift and interprets for his clients. Previously, he served as executive vice president at Interscope Geffen A&M Records and was a manager for hip hop artist Nas and R&B singer Mary J. Blige. He has helped his clients translate their visions into lucrative deals and partnerships to make their dreams come to pass. If you have skills like Joseph or Steve, as a 2man, you must be motivated by transforming the vision of your organization into a reality.

The Kyrie Effect

One of the motivations for writing this book and starting the 2man coaching network is because I've seen great 2s leave their spots to become ordinary 1s. In 2017, after reaching the NBA Finals for three straight years and winning one championship due to him hitting the biggest shot of his career, Cleveland Cavaliers point guard Kyrie Irving (who, coincidentally, wore the #2 jersey) decided he no longer wanted to play 2man to the greatest player on the planet, Lebron James.

It was public knowledge that Irving was demanding a trade to a team where he could be "The Man," or the #1. Social media and all the sports outlets went crazy, and many people questioned why he would leave a situation where he was on one of the best teams in the league every year and that allowed him to play with someone who made the game easy for him. In an interview on ESPN's *First Take*, Irving said he just wanted to be in a place where he was happy and could lead a team. He was asked, "Is it more important for you to be the man [#1] or to win championships?" and "You know things won't be as easy as they were in Cleveland because of the attention Lebron required, right?"

The jury is still out on if Irving can lead his new team to a championship, but the fact is that before Lebron joined the Cavs, when Irving was #1, the team was one of the worst in the league. Will Irving succeed as a 1? Can he make his teammates better? Can he be as great as he was when all the attention and double teams weren't focused on him? Time will tell, but it has been proven that he excelled in his role as a 2man and has the jewelry to prove it.

My point? Be careful of jumping out of place and desiring a position that you may not be called or equipped to handle. If you're producing fruit in your role as a 2man, your team is winning, and you're being recognized for your contributions, then maybe you should consider blooming where you're planted and allow God to open up other opportunities and challenges for growth without having to demand a trade.

HOW TO FIND A 2

Terry Nance, author of *God's Armor Bearer*, says, "Today, apostles, prophets, evangelists, pastors and teachers all across our land are crying out for a man like Joshua to come to their aid."[1] He listed a few actions leaders could take when looking for help.

1. Pray for God's divinely appointed people to come your way.
2. Be willing to invest yourself in the lives of your helpers.
3. Delegate authority.
4. Look for the spirit of an armor-bearer in people.

In *How to Lead When You're Not in Charge*, Clay Scroggins talks about how to leverage influence when you lack authority. In an interview with his senior pastor, Andy Stanley, Scroggins says, "We are all in charge of something, so begin there and make it as great as possible. [Ask] What am I in charge of? and create an oasis of excellence there. . . . How can I lead when I don't have all the authority? is a bad question."[2] After listening to Nance and Scroggins and thinking about my own experiences, I believe there are two ways to find your 2man.

Found in the House

The first way to find a 2 is to find him or her in the house. Potiphar of Egypt found Joseph working in the house. Joshua, Moses' successor, was serving in the house in a totally unrelated capacity. Barnabas saw what was happening, jumped in, and was a top giver in the early church, which made him get noticed. These were people who served in the house and served with an attitude of anything, everything, or nothing at all. Lonnell Williams, one of my ministry partners, is a perfect example.

Lonnell came to our church as an intern while working on his master's degree at nearby Princeton University. He would ask to sit in on executive meetings when, normally, others weren't invited to. He took on whatever tasks other people didn't want. He also asked my pastor what he was reading and would then come back having read the entire book in a week. Lonnell moved from intern to ministry assistant to administrative assistant to executive assistant to the pastor's first assistant to director of ministries—and the titles just kept coming.

Lonnell now lives in Atlanta and handles investment accounts for millionaires. This young man was found in the house; became a son of the house, as Layne Schranz mentioned; and is currently working on his first book, *Anything, Everything, or Nothing at All*.

Those sitting around waiting for a title will never be a leader's right 2man. The right people don't need a title to take charge. If they are asked to close the store in your absence, not only do they close the store, but they stay late to do inventory to make things easier for the next staff shift in the morning. If you ask them to serve on the parking lot, they show up early and lead by example. If they are on your ministerial staff, they show up at funerals when no one else does and volunteer to read the Old and New Testament passages, or they submit suggestions on how to improve the congregational care system.

When trying to identify your 2man in your organization, find out who is leading without the authority, and you may have found your person. When you hear people say, "I would have helped out, but no one asked me," let them stay right where they are. I subscribe to the philosophy that some people don't get involved because they haven't been asked, and if we as leaders want to get more volunteers, then we should make the big ask. But that doesn't apply for potential seconds-in-command. They aren't waiting. They are like the horse in the stable waiting to get out!

Found by Referral

The other way to find a 2man is by referral, which is beneficial because others close to you who know you and your challenges may know someone who would fit your needs and be compatible with you. (By the way, everyone has "a guy"!) Referrals also are good because when your potential 2men come by referral of your core team, it minimizes some of the drama that you are sure to experience later, such as territorialism, jealousy, and insecurities from current team members (which creates challenges I'll discuss later). Let me share a few stories of some great support leaders found in my favorite book.

There was an Egyptian king who needed someone who could help him save his nation from suffering during an upcoming recession. While he couldn't quite understand the meaning of his nightmares, which were forecasting the future trouble, he asked members of his staff for help. They couldn't help him, but they knew about "a guy" who had a troubled past but who was gifted in that area. The king sought out this man named Joseph, and his business prospered.

There was another leader who was having mental health challenges that were driving him mad. Members of his staff knew he needed help, so they referred to him a young, gifted musician who they thought could help him. They requested for him to play for their boss, and his music soothed the leader so much that the musician became the leader's armor-bearer. The musician's name was David.

Finally, there was a king in ancient Iraq who had disturbing dreams that no one could interpret. He was so bothered by them that he threatened to kill all of his staff members if they couldn't help him. In fear, his team sought out a foreigner who happened to be working there, and they referred him to the king. Daniel not only interpreted the dreams, but he also helped four kings run their entire operations because he was a H.O.R.S.E.

Leaders, if you can't find someone in the house to raise up to serve as your 2man, then share your need with members of your inner circle and have them recommend someone who will fit your needs.

Life Change

How I became Executive Pastor at Change Church is an interesting story. For six years, I had been leading and operating BNB Consulting & Associates, the business I founded based out of Houston. This was initially a side business I created in response to a need to help a few artists in their entertainment careers. But the business grew from managing artists to consulting with small businesses, nonprofit organizations, and churches.

In 2005, I decided to step out on faith and launch my company full-time. While building my clientele in Houston, one of my independent contractors just happened to be building a website for Change Church (formerly known as Kingdom Church), which had just started a new ministry right outside of Trenton, New Jersey. While hearing the pastor's story and needs for his fast-growing church, the independent contractor heard him say that he needed help with organizational development and building a staff that could help him. Before you know it, Dharius Daniels was calling my office to talk about his needs and find out about our services. After a few site visits and assessments, we began working together contractually.

In 2009, after a few years of putting strong systems in place, developing job descriptions, staffing key positions, and working on improving the overall experience, the weirdest thing happened. I was called to the teaching ministry while in a Bible study Pastor Daniels was teaching, and everything changed. Before I knew it, I went from outside consultant to a son in the ministry and director of ministry operations (later, to the role of executive pastor).

All of this happened because of a referral. Someone knew my work and professionalism and heard the need of this young pastor halfway across the country and connected us. Like Joseph, Daniel, and David, I am now the 2man serving and submitting to my pastor. I went from a Consultant/Friend to an Executioner/Interpreter with the assignment of not letting any of his words fall to the ground.

So to the senior leaders looking for your 2s, remember that you will find them already leading in your organization, or you will find them by referral. Either way, keep your eyes open and your ears receptive to how they may come. But remember, help is on the way!

---

[1] *God's Armor Bearer: Serving God's Leaders*, by Terry Nance (Spirit Filled Books, 2003); page 55.

[2] "How to Build Your Influence," by Clay Scroggins on The EntreLeadership Podcast #240 (https://itunes.apple.com/us/podcast/the-entreleadership-podcast/id435836905?mt=2&i=1000398830502).

HOW TO TRAIN 2S

ou've been selected for this role. You understand who you are and what the role requires, and you have the qualities necessary to be a solid 2man. The next step is to receive proper training. I recommend to 1s that they initially train 2s as they would train all new employees, new members, and leaders.

My pastor, Dr. Dharius Daniels, did an excellent job mapping out our orientation process that we follow. The process includes sessions on understanding our church, learning about its history and its vision, going through our vision strategy, and understanding our philosophy of ministry. Then we help new employees understand their individual callings and how they align with our ministry, character, and culture. Culture is everything, so it's important for 2men to embrace and embody the culture of the organization because they must model that for everyone else.

Finally, we emphasize the need for attention to detail, what excellence looks like in our context, and how to understand our #1. The Bible says, "And we beseech you, brethren, to know them which labour among you, and are over you in the Lord, and admonish you" (1 Thessalonians 5:12, KJV).

Don't underestimate the need for this last instruction, because just as important as it is for you as a 2man to know who you are, in order to be a great help to your leader, you need to know who he or she is. Pastor Daniels is a Joshua-type personality, an apostolic leader, a visionary, a teacher, a coach, a strategist, and a delegator. In order for me to help him execute the vision, I need to know as much about him as possible so that I can complement him.

The Spirit Transfer

After 2men are properly orientated, they need specific training and an opportunity to shadow their #1s so that the spirit and the DNA of their leaders can be imparted to them. This is what I call "the spirit transfer." Numbers 11:25 (KJV) says, "The LORD came down in a cloud, and spake unto him, and took of the spirit that was upon him, and gave it unto the seventy elders: and it came to pass, that, when the spirit rested upon them, they prophesied, and did not cease."

In her book *Loyalty*, Jacquetta Smith gives excellent pointers for helping 2men receive a successful spirit transfer.[1]

1. Read your CEO's work (letters, memos, brochures, for example). This will give you a clear idea of the pastor's writing style. It will also give you the direction on the heartthrob of the pastor.
2. Watch your pastor closely, watching for his or her mannerisms. How does your pastor make decisions, and what standards does he or she use? How does your pastor handle other people, handle pressure, and interact with his or her family?
3. Execute according to your pastor's style. A leader should know how to execute assignments the way the pastor wants things to happen.
4. Know your leader's likes and dislikes.

I first stepped into the 2man role at my first church in Houston, Texas. My pastor took a Jesus-type approach to training me. Once my pastor discovered who I was and what I did by profession (management and budget analyst, with community outreach skills), he did what Jesus did to His disciples.

In Matthew 4:19, Jesus calls his disciples to Him, not to a specific assignment. This is a critical point in Jesus' discipleship plan and is key for 1s in training 2s. Jesus invited His disciples to follow Him (step 1) and told them He would make them fishers of men (step 2). Before Jesus ever gave them an assignment, He had them to spend time with Him. They ate with Him, traveled with Him, watched Him do his job, talked with Him about what they experienced, and discussed His thought process related to why He did what He did.

My pastor didn't give me an orientation manual and a binder filled with information on organizational procedures. He called me to walk with him. He asked me to come to his house to have dinner with his wife and children and to talk. He would talk to me for hours about vision, how he saw the ministry running, and the type of people he would need to help the vision come to pass. He talked to me about the five-fold vision that was bigger than the church but included a community development corporation, a school, a media ministry, and a consulting arm.

On other occasions, my pastor asked me to drive him and accompany him to his many speaking engagements. While at those church services, I was to observe and listen to the conversations that he had with other pastors. Then, for example, he would ask me what I observed in how different churches conducted their services or how they kept their facilities. This was all part of his calling me to him before he gave me any assignments. He was putting his DNA and his spirit into me before giving me any church-related tasks.

Finally, my pastor started putting my gifts and talents to work by inviting me to church planning meetings and telling me to make notes. Then he asked for my suggestions on how we could administrate certain projects, such as managing our database or printing our bulletins. Once I gave suggestions, he gave me the task to make sure it happened, and then he gave me contact people to call at other churches to see how they did things and who they used. So, again, I went from driver to financial administrator to community developer to deacon and all the way to COO. But my pastor was testing me with small projects because he knew that it was best that I be faithful over a few things before he could entrust me with more.

Three Types of Knowledge

In addition to the DNA of the leader, I also believe there is certain knowledge that a 2man must obtain as part of the training. When I teach my *Transforming Visions Into Realities* seminars to leaders, I talk about how the key to obtaining excellence requires three types of knowledge. The same principles apply here.

Internal knowledge is understanding how the organization works, how to get things done, and knowing the standing operating procedures. *External knowledge* is benchmarking other organizations that do what you do, reading or listening to books, and attending trainings. *Spiritual knowledge* is what happens in your devotional time. If you work in the church arena, then you must spend time with God in order to be successful, because some of the best ideas and strategies will come directly from Him. Don't rely on your pastor to do all of your studying and reading, but fill your well so that you have more to talk about.

Critical Success Tools

In addition to the training needed for a 2man, there are other critical tools a 2man needs in order to do his or her job at a high level.

Clarity. This is the most important and valuable gift your leader can give you. Being clear on the vision, the expectations, the goals and objectives, and the dos and don'ts will help you survive and thrive in this role.

Support. Serving in a 2man role isn't easy. Sometimes we have to be the bad cop, the bearer of bad news, and the leader they love to hate. So it's important that we have support from the top when we are going out to the wolves.

Honesty. As a 2man, if you're going down the wrong path, not doing well, or your leader wants something more out of you, then they need to be honest and let you know. My pastor had to deal with me about a situation that occurred with one of my lead staff ministers. I became too casual and comfortable with this minister and the minister's spouse, and some of our discussions in a social environment were made known to my pastor. He had to be honest with me and correct me so that my good wouldn't be spoken of as evil. I appreciated his honesty, and the situation made me use even more discretion about which people I allowed in my private space.

Direct communication. In order to execute your #1's directives, you need direct communication and not second-hand information where the message can be filtered or altered. Think of your #1 as a military general who gives direct orders in a war. If we as 2s are responsible for carrying out the execution of a plan, then that information should come straight from the top and not from one of your leader's subordinates.

Leadership. We are called to serve our #1s, but we are not just workers to carry out the mission. Instead, we should be objects of the mission. We need to be led, we need to be pastored, and we need to be fathered in ministry. At our church, we are called to change lives, so I don't just want to help change others and not be changed myself.

Resources. In order to be effective, we need to be equipped with personal and organizational resources so that money is never our concern (to the best of the organization's ability) and so that we can carry out our jobs. Don't send me into a gun fight with a knife and expect a favorable outcome. I've had some David situations where I've had to kill bears and lions (enemies to the vision) with my bare hands or a butter knife, but please don't make this a habit for your #2s. I still have the scars from those battles. Suitable resources also include coaching, consulting, and conferences being made available so 2s can keep their axes sharp.

Flexibility. Leaders have to decide how best to use their #2s and what main goals need to be accomplished. A great 2man is always on call and ready to move at any time when needed (H.O.R.S.E.). Many times, 2s are in the office more than the 1s, which is part of the job. So hounding 2s about being in the office from 9-5 and taking only an hour for lunch probably isn't the best use of their skills and talents. As 2s, flexibility is key because if we are traveling with our #1s, staying late to handle board meetings in their absence, attending all church services so we can make sure everyone else is doing their jobs, then we need time to pull away to pick up our children from school, take vacations, and run errands between meetings.

Public affirmation of delegated authority. I have seen many mistakes made by other 1s in not providing this affirmation. If the 2man is going to have authority, then the team and those involved need to hear the leader publicly declare it. It wasn't by accident that Pharaoh gave Joseph a chariot, another robe, and a signature ring in front of everyone. He was making a public declaration that Joseph was in charge and delineating what exactly was under his authority so there wouldn't be any division or confusion.

Managing Power and Authority

In conclusion, I'll say a few words on the need for 2s to manage power and delegated authority properly. We have to view power and authority with the right perspective and lens. As 2s, we aren't given power for the sake of power, but we're bestowed with power so we can steward the vision and execute the goals of our leaders without hindrance.

Potiphar gave Joseph authority after he proved himself and for his own personal benefit. When the apostles called for the first deacons, the apostles delegated authority so they could focus on their primary responsibility, which was the ministry of the Word. So don't deceive yourself when given power, because the power isn't for you. You have received power so you can carry out what you have been called to do.

Think of the term *steward*, which is a person who manages another's property and/or financial affairs or one who administers anything as the agent of another. As 2men, we are stewards of the authority given to us, and we have to administer it wisely. Failure to manage power and authority appropriately is putting a date on your calendar for being dismissed from your role because your #1's voice and credibility with the people is his greatest asset. If he loses that because of your arrogance and abuse and mismanagement of power, then you are no longer an asset but a liability.

One day while working in my 2man role with my first pastor, we had to evacuate Houston because of an incoming hurricane. We loaded up the church vehicles with all critical files and equipment, got our families together, and prepared to evacuate.

What was normally a four-hour drive from Houston to Dallas took us 24 hours because of all the traffic and pandemonium. In the course of our trip, I ended up driving my #1's Mercedes, and one of the other leaders drove my truck. At some point, I fell asleep driving his car, and I nicked another car, although the damage wasn't too bad. The leader driving my truck fell asleep and ran my truck off the road and totaled it. Luckily, no one was injured, and we all survived and made it to our destination.

When we returned home, we were laughing about the incident, but my pastor then flipped the conversation and made a valuable point as it related to my role as a 2man and the other leader's responsibility to help us achieve the vision without destroying it. He said, "Let me wreck my own car!" He was talking about the vehicle, but I also heard him clearly as it relates to the power and authority that had been delegated to me. If you are given power and authority, then use it wisely and don't wreck it!

---

[1]Adapted from *Loyalty*; page 55.

CHAPTER EIGHT
WHAT ABOUT ME?
THE CHALLENGES OF BEING A 2

This may be the most important chapter of this book because I have seen how failure in managing this area has destroyed great 2s, and my prayer is that it never happens to another one of us. There are so many challenges that come with this role, including isolation, jealousy and envy from team members, successful management of our ambition, limited spousal support or pressure from them for us to pursue other career paths, a lack of outlets for us to vent, and a neglect of self-care. There are also the struggles with right motives and unmet needs, which can destroy us, too.

Who Do You Think You Are?

Another challenge that a 2man must deal with is when people ask, "Who do you think you are?" implying that they question us as the delegated authority. Do you remember when you were in high school and you walked in the room only to find that your favorite teacher wasn't there and had been replaced by a substitute? You and your friends probably exclaimed, "Yes! Free day today because we don't have to do anything this person says." That's what it feels like to be a 2man when we're put in charge by the senior leader without proper introduction and role clarity—minus the paper wads being thrown at our backs.

How do you handle the challenges when other team members don't know you or know why you are there? They have been accustomed to getting information and instructions firsthand from the leader's mouth, and now they have to listen to you say, "I need your weekly productivity report by Friday close of business" or "This is how we are going to handle staff meetings moving forward." Immediately, you will be challenged with statements such as "Oh, I already know what to do," "I have been here since day one, and we normally do things a certain way," or the dreaded "I know what Pastor wants."

There are a multitude of ways to handle these challenges. Most leadership book writers will tell you that influential power is better than positional power. So that means you can't walk in like Eddie Murphy from the movie *48 Hours*, yelling, "There's a new sheriff in town, and his name is Reggie Hammond" after shooting the place up. (Actually, I would have liked to have done that in some of my previous experiences.)

But the best and most effective way to handle challenges from others is for your senior leader to introduce you and explain why you are there, what your responsibility is, and how he or she needs staff members and others to work with you to accomplish the mission, with a reminder that any disrespect will not be tolerated. This is called public affirmation and proper delegation of authority. If you can get this from your leader, then you have the foundation to build with confidence. If you can't get this, then start taking lessons at the local shooting range (LOL).

You only have a certain amount of time to lean on your positional power and show the team how competent and effective you are. That public affirmation doesn't last long. Just ask Jesus! When He was baptized by his cousin John, His Heavenly Father affirmed Him in front of the entire crowd. The people clapped and were amazed for a while, until He started stepping on their toes and moving in on some of their territory. So when you get in the spot, be ready to be a H.O.R.S.E. Time is not your friend.

What About My Dreams?

The next challenge is answering the question you might ask yourself, *What do I do with my own vision, dreams, and aspirations?* On multiple occasions along this journey, I have had to wrestle with my own desires, ambitions, and dreams that I knew were from God.

My story may be a little different from most because I started and ran my own management and consulting firm where I was the boss, the #1. I launched BNB Consulting & Associates after I was already serving in a 2man capacity in my role as management analyst for the Environmental Protection Agency and assisting my pastor. A few years before taking a leap of faith to pursue my company full-time, I shared with my pastor that I felt God leading me to help churches and businesses all over the country. Since our ministry was growing by leaps and bounds, we mutually decided that it wasn't the right time, so I sat on the vision for years. It wasn't until the church was reaching its seventh year that I felt the urgency to move forward.

Years later, after serving in my first stint as 2man at Change Church, I felt led to shut down the company to focus on helping Pastor Daniels fulfill his vision of changing as many lives as possible. When I began pondering this decision, I discussed it with my dad, my mentors, and my wife. One of my spiritual mentors gave me the word that I needed: " 'Truly I tell you,' Jesus said to them, 'no one who has left home or wife or brothers or sisters or parents or children for the sake of the kingdom of God will fail to receive many times as much in this age, and in the age to come eternal life' " (Luke 18:29-30). I found great comfort in this, and I hope I can bring a sense of encouragement to those of you with your own dreams. God promises that when you sacrifice for the sake of the Kingdom and for others, you will be rewarded in this lifetime.

When you lay your dreams on the altar of sacrifice, it isn't easy at the time. I felt like Abraham going to the mountain to kill his long-awaited and promised son. The positive side of it has been that I have been able to see God's promises fulfilled in my life in ways I couldn't have imagined, and my pastor has been the biggest supporter of me launching this new initiative. (Actually, he was the one who told me that it was time for me to start writing this book.)

My entire goal with my company was to help leaders to identify, interpret, and strategically transform their dreams into realities. We did that through consulting leaders with a focus on organizational development, staff and leadership development, and branding. To my surprise, I am now doing the same things in a different format through my nonprofit organization; my church; and my pastor's coaching program, 180 Network, where I contribute leadership.

Many other pastors have become aware of my gifting as well, and I am frequently booked to go into churches to develop their leaders and consult with them on best practices in growing their ministries. I also probably wouldn't be writing this book and coaching executive leaders through www.2mansupport.com if I hadn't decided to put my ambitions and dreams in God's hands and trust that He was concerned about me.

Derrick Noble

There is one person above all I look up to as a mentor, example, and friend in this 2man arena. He is one of the two people I frequently speak of when sharing my heart for this 2man movement and one of the ones I called over ten years ago to discuss it with. He has so much experience and knowledge to share, in particular on the challenges of being a 2man. His name is Derrick Noble, and he serves as Chief of Staff to Bishop Joseph W. Walker III, presiding Bishop of Full Gospel Baptist Church Fellowship International.

Derrick has served in various capacities in his role with Bishop Walker in Nashville, Tennessee, over the past 12 years. But before serving in his present role, he served as executive administrator for Bishop Clarence McClendon in Los Angeles. When I asked Derrick what advice he would give to a new 2man coming into the role, he said, "Be sure to make time for self-care. It's important for the 2man or woman to schedule time to disconnect and refresh. Not intentionally making time for self-care is a set-up for self-destruction and burnout."

I look up to this man because he has been there and done it. When you retire from a role and others seek you out because you did it so well, then I think your voice warrants attention. Derrick's words are golden to me, so I wanted to make sure I shared some of his almost 30 years of 2man experience with you. When I asked him why people don't last long in these positions, he attributed it to "stress, burn-out, lack of appreciation, and no longer being graced for the assignment."

How Is Your Mental Health?

Speaking of self-care, other challenges 2men have to overcome are those with their mental and emotional health. My wife is a mental health therapist and helps me understand this area even more.

As a 2, you have committed to take on every other task that the 1 would be doing if it were not for you. This means that you may have a laundry list of things to do that, depending on the infrastructure, may include, but are not limited to, acting as liaison between other leaders (keeping him or her abreast of current operation intel); acting as a buffer between staff members; overseeing day-to-day business operations; reviewing the financial health of the organization and forecasting budgets; performing pastoral care (or overseeing the process); being a community relationship builder; and acting as emergency contact, confidant, and muscle.

In the eyes of the people, you are next in command for *every-thing*. When people think of their needs and operational aspects, they think of you (if you are effective in your role, of course). With this laundry list of responsibility also comes the weight and the need to be effective in work/life balance.

There are several studies that show clergies' risk of emotional health challenges is far greater than others. Duke Divinity School conducted a study in 2008 that showed rates for clergy as doubled that of the then-national rates of depression. This same study also showed that anxiety was also essentially high in comparison to other numbers, most notably due to job stress. I would also argue that those who are in positions such as ours are not just struggling emotionally but also physically due to lack of proper sleep, rest, eating healthy, and physical exercise.

Simply put, with everything going on in the life of a 2, self-care just doesn't seem to fit. As a result, while the organization may be thriving and evolving, we are or may be moving toward mentally and physically breaking down. This may be hard to hear and digest because in your mind you may be thinking, *I'm great at everything else. Certainly, I'm great in this area, too.* I dare you to take time to stop and investigate it. That's why I believe this resource is so valuable to you. Others have hit brick walls so you don't have to.

You may be saying to yourself, *I don't see how any of this is applicable to me. I'm not suffering.* Perhaps you're not, but is your pastor suffering? Are other clergy under your care suffering? In a 2016 report, The Gospel Coalition (TGC) reported that "more than half of Evangelical and Reformed pastors told the Schaeffer Institute in 2015 and 2016 that although they're happier (79 percent), they don't have any good and true friends (58 percent). About the same number reported they can't meet their church's unrealistic expectations (52 percent). And close to a third battle discouragement (34 percent) or depression/the fear of inadequacy (35 percent) on a regular basis."[1]

In our role as 2s, safe spaces are hard to find. And even when you discover them, you will find yourself being cautious what you share because you have been groomed to cover, so you still carry weight. Senior leaders and executive support leaders are just as suicidal and mentally and emotionally unstable as those they lead.

What can we as 2s do to take better care of ourselves and bear up under the pressures we face? Consider the following suggestions[2]:

- First, seek counseling. This is going to require work, venturing outside of your comfort zone and interviewing counselors until you get the right fit. And it's also going to take a great level of vulnerability and trust.
- Create for yourself a sabbath, a 24-hour period where you are not engaging in anything work-related. Set aside time for yourself.
- Develop good sleep habits. Research shows that anything less than four hours a night for extended periods of time can lead to irritability, lack of focus and productivity, anxiousness, increased fatigue, and increased stress, which can induce other health complications.
- Attend to medical concerns immediately and effectively.
- Develop a regular eating schedule (make better food choices) and a workout regimen that is effective for you (for example, yoga, aerobics, HIIT, kickboxing, cycling, or walking) at least three times per week.
- If you are married and have children, restructure your schedule so that you can invest time with those

you love and who love you back. When your home life is good and you feel supported, appreciated, and attended to, then you will be that much more effective in your role as a 2man. You get out of it what you put into it. "Water your grass, and watch it grow."

I hope this give you greater insight into at least some of the things that you, or others you serve with, can do in order to get in front of these challenges before they get started. These and other issues must be properly addressed and dealt with for us to be effective and efficient in the roles in which we are called to serve. I pray that we take our families, our self-care, and our issues seriously and do the work necessary to allow us to flourish and be fruitful as 2men and women. If you want the help, then our network will be a resource that will be available to you as we walk through these deep waters together.

---

[1]"Why Pastors Are Committing Suicide," by Sarah Eekhoff Zylstra for The Gospel Coalition, November 23, 2016 (https://www.thegospelcoalition.org/article why-pastors-are-committing-suicide/).
[2]Contributed by Verily Harper, LPC.

CHAPTER NINE

THE 2MAN AND HIS FAMILY

S erving as a 2man doesn't just impact you and your organization, but it also affects your family. Derrick Noble says
that one of the most challenging aspects in his role is being
unable to consistently give time and attention to what matters most to his family.

Before I became a 2man at Change Church, I was working
with my pastor as a consultant. In 2007, at a Bible study Pastor
Daniels was teaching, I was called into the teaching ministry, and
everything shifted. I went from being a consultant and an interpreter to my pastor to being a son of the house who needed
him. All of this would totally change me and my family forever.

In 2009, my family and I moved from Houston to New Jersey
to serve in a new capacity. I felt God was not only calling me to
ministry but was calling my family as well, and it required me to
shut down everything that I had going on. After years of building
a company, being the #1, employing others, providing contract
work for a lot of people, providing for my family, and building a
unique boutique consulting firm, I was now about to sacrifice
it all to be a 2man for someone else. Sounds admirable, right?

Of course, it wouldn't, it shouldn't, it couldn't be that easy,
not when dealing with Kingdom work. My family and I moved to
New Jersey, but I had to leave two of my daughters behind. We
have a blended family, so in total, we have four children (but
that's a topic for a whole different book). My family was now
separated. My wife and her children were living in a new place
completely across the country and separate from their comfort
zone; and I was working for someone else, trying to make his
vision a reality.

I was on salary, making considerably less. The living expense difference between Houston, Texas, and Princeton, New Jersey, is like night and day; and my wife had had to leave her job to follow me. So there were all sorts of dynamics that we weren't ready for, and initially it created a lot of tension in our marriage. Your story may not be like mine, but you will still need to prepare for the warfare that is coming your way through your family by accepting the call to be a 2man. There are several pointers I can give you to help you balance your family and be a good 2.

First, make sure you and your spouse are on the same page as it relates to the calling and assignment on your life, preferably before you get married if at all possible. If it's too late for that, then it's time to sit down and have real conversations about who you are and where you see yourself going in the future. Some of the most challenging discussions I've had with 2s that have nearly brought me to tears haven't been about hearing their ambitions to be the top leader, but about their spouses' ambitions and expectations.

Our spouses see how great and smart we are. But if their ambitions for us aren't managed properly, they will say things such as "You are smarter than he is." "You could have done a better job in handling that than she did." "If you were in charge, things would be better." As 2s, if we aren't careful, we will start believing the hype and find ourselves discontent in our role. And then the divide starts.

The problems start rather innocently and seductively; but in the end, it's similar to when Eve influenced Adam to eat the forbidden fruit. But the fruit wasn't the real problem. The real problem was in the disobedience of what God told Adam to do. Adam's passiveness in shutting down the enemy's voice was what got him fired. So make sure your spouse is on the same page with you and understands the role and how important it is that he or she supports it fully before you accept. If you are content in being an Armor-Bearer, a Consultant, a Friend, an Interpreter, an Executioner, or a Partner and don't desire anything more, then your spouse must accept and embrace that, or none of this will work.

Second, give more effort and attention to your spouse and family than you ever have before. Serving as a 2man means you become a suitable helpmeet to your leader, much in the way we expect a wife to be. Therefore, your family can't be made to feel that you appreciate, sacrifice, love, and serve your #1 and his family more than you do your own.

In our armor bearer/personal assistant training manual, Pastor Daniels makes it clear that "each service that you render to a servant in God's church is a service you need to render to your mate. For example, if you help your leader put on his coat, then you should also be helping your wife put on her coat. You should carry her bags and open her door. Why? This is necessary, first, because your home is your first ministry. Second, it is a teaching tool that helps you become what you do. Service to your mate also teaches you how to serve beyond the flesh. Relational difficulties will often make it difficult to serve your mate in this way, but we are called to serve regardless of how we feel. Finally, serving your mate helps minimize the manifestation of jealousy that can be a result of you demonstrating a care and a reverence for someone else over and above them."

In other words, you can't give the enemy any room to mess up what the Lord is calling you to do. At one point, your spouse may have been "the first lady" and was the center of attention. But now she is "the second lady." Is there even such a thing as that? Part of the reason I started www.2mansupport.com is to ensure we are able to deal with some of these dynamics in a safe environment and also to provide support to our spouses.

My wife has had to serve with me in these capacities in multiple locations, so she is well equipped to speak to others. I have watched her sacrifice, experience and overcome depression, work to find her sweet spot, and find significance in her place; and she looks forward to sharing her story with others through this network. In no way do we feel as if we have mastered this; but we feel as if we can share our experiences, and together we can all support one another.

Third, set balance and boundaries by developing an annual, quarterly, monthly, weekly, and daily plan; and then communicate that with your family. For example, after I work with my #1 to set our organization's calendar in place for the upcoming year that includes his vacation time, planned conferences, special events, and church activities, then the very next thing I do is start mapping out my own family's schedule so that it doesn't conflict with his.

My wife and I discuss what we want to do and when would be the best times for me to take off to do those things. We consider dates such as the week of our wedding anniversary, the weekends surrounding our birthdays, the weeks that the kids will be on spring break, the holidays for the year, our summer vacation, and if we will be taking some stay-cations, for example. I then block those weeks and days off and let my #1 know about them as well.

I've also learned to think on a quarterly schedule because it's important that I take a few personal days off to recoup. And at this stage in my career, I need sabbaticals similar to what my #1 does but for shorter periods of time. I make sure that each month I am aware of special days for my family, such as birthdays, holidays, and the kids' extracurricular activities so that those things have my attention and are scheduled so that I don't miss them.

Finally, I sit down with my family and map out what a normal week looks like for us. Jeff Smith, who was once an assistant to his pastor, Bishop Michael Pitts, gives this advice: "Make the most of moments, look for opportunities to make memories, keep priorities in order, and remember that seasons with spouse and family only come once."

I have finally found a rhythm that works for us, and I encourage all of my team members and 2s that I coach to do this on the front end versus the back end. We have to map out when our long days in the office will be, which helps our family know when we will be home late. We map out when our weekly date night is, which may include going out or just watching a movie at home alone. We map out when family night is when we do something as an entire family. I even go as far as mapping out my "me time," which is typically Saturday mornings when I can complete the tasks on my honey-do list, wash the cars, or just sit around in my pajamas and look at the ceiling fan go around and around.

More recently, with help from my #1 and my personal coach, I have made it a priority to set aside a time frame that is my personal sabbath. It begins on Sunday afternoon after church and goes for a 24-hour period the next day. This has been the greatest gift that I have ever given to myself, my family, and my ministry. You have to set some form of structure in place so that your family has consistency and so they see themselves as priority, not just from your mouth but on your calendar.

THINGS 2S WANT 1S TO KNOW

P astor Daniels and I thought it would be good to end this book with a chapter on things we as 2s want our 1s to know. Serving in the second chair, second seat, second chariot—whatever category we want to call it—isn't easy. As you probably know by now, it requires sacrifice, humility, good health, submission, and a harnessing of ambition. Second place is never the desired outcome from anyone looking to be successful. But I pray that after you've read this book, you see that it's not about one person winning and another one losing. Instead, it's about winning for the sake of the Kingdom so we can make an impact.

"It takes two to make things go right," but there are some things that we want our leaders to know. This list is not in order of importance, but all of these thoughts are honest. We believe they will be helpful to 1s who have a great 2 on their side who may not have shared these things, or this list will help 1s who are looking for someone to come alongside and help them fulfill the vision.

I've shared some of these thoughts to Pastor Daniels, and some of them I haven't said—but now he knows. Some of the thoughts are from the current incredible 2s who contributed to this work. So, again, I thank them because they are doing major work in the Kingdom, and we appreciate them taking time out to be interviewed for this book.

Here's what 2s want 1s to know:

- We believe in you 100 percent, or else we wouldn't be doing this.
- We want you to believe in us 100 percent.
- As we lift up your hands, its challenging because more than likely we have no one to lift ours.

- We need sabbaticals and extended periods of rest just as you do.
- We have no outlet because we are your confidant and secret-bearer, which means we can't share anything with our spouses or those we oversee, so we need resources like www.2mansupport.com.
- Please don't ever embarrass us or shame us in public or in front of the staff because it renders us powerless and ineffective when dealing with those you want us to manage.
- When you allow others to come to you and skip the chain of command, it renders us powerless.
- We understand that at times our role is to play bad cop to your good cop. Nobody likes a bad cop. But as long as we have your support, we can be effective.
- Help us help you!
- Reciprocate the support. If we are bringing relief to you, then when possible, ask how you can reciprocate the relief.
- See us. In other words, see the hard work and dedication that we are putting in to make your life easier.
- Like Aretha Franklin sang, "R-E-S-P-E-C-T. Find out what it means to me."
- Honor the gifts and callings on our lives as we make it our top priority to honor the ones on yours.
- Don't forget to pastor and lead us because we need to be the benefactors of the vision that God has given you for everyone else.
- When you are making moves and decisions, consider us and the impact that it will have on us and our families. It may not alter your decision, but at least consider us.
- The more clarity you give us on what your expectations, goals, objectives, needs, and wants are, then the better we can help you execute them.

- Clear communication is a benefit and an essential element for a second chair who wants to build and maintain a healthy relationship with the first chair. (See *Leading From the Second Chair: Serving Your Church, Fulfilling Your Role, and Realizing Your Dreams*, by Mike Bonem and Roger Patterson.)
- We love you and your family.
- We're thankful for the trust you have in us and for giving us the keys to Christ's church.
- We're loyal.
- We are here with you, and we are thankful that you have allowed us to grow, make mistakes, and learn from you.
- You have been as loyal to us as we have been to you.
- We appreciate what God has done in allowing us to work with you in building the Kingdom.
- We are called to you, not the city or the church. God builds His kingdom relationally, not locationally.
- Remain open to ideas and sound advice we offer you.
- Remain open when we inform you of an urging that the end of our assignment is approaching. Commit to working with us to find the best person to fill the vacancy.
- Balance is critical!
- Input and encouragement are always valued.
- Your boldness and our strategizing; your urgency and our patience; your spirit and our natural; your vision and our leadership; your strengths and our weaknesses; your weaknesses and our strengths. Us having a great understanding of this because many don't.

CHAPTER ELEVEN

PERSPECTIVE OF A 1: AN INTERVIEW WITH DR. DHARIUS DANIELS

F or this final chapter, I interviewed Dr. Dharius Daniels, founder and lead pastor of Change Church, based in Ewing, New Jersey. Dr. Daniels has a doctorate's degree in leadership; leads a multi-site church with campuses in New Jersey and California, with one soon coming to Florida; has authored multiple books and resources; speaks nationally and internationally in churches, universities, and conferences; has his own television broadcast that reaches millions of people; and oversees 180 Network, a coaching network of almost 30 pastors from all over the world. I felt it would be remiss of me not to sit down with him and get his insight and perspectives on this book. Here are his thoughts as a 1.

Ramone Harper: What are the greatest challenges 1s face?

Dr. Dharius Daniels: The challenges that leaders face will vary according to the personality makeup, natural skill set, and spiritual gifting of that specific leader. There are times when we struggle with clarity of mission, staying on mission, and strategically navigating through all the competing responsibilities that can distract us from our mission. However, one of the greatest challenges we face is discovering, developing, and deploying the right team. In the words of Jim Collins, we need the right people on the bus and the right people in the right seats. It takes teamwork to make the dream work. Therefore, finding the person or people who can help implement and oversee the vision can be quite challenging.

Harper: In your own words, how would you define a 2man?

Daniels: First, I want to reiterate that the term *2man* isn't gender exclusive. I would consider my wife a 2man. Second, I would contend that a 2man isn't just one person. There were times in the life of our organization when different people carried similar responsibilities that were equally important. The overall idea of the "It Takes Two" concept is that it takes more than one person, so any person who helps carry a lion's share of the load of the organization could be considered a 2. They add value to the organization and the senior leader where it is needed most. But what they do, where they sit on the organizational chart, and what their titles are will vary.

Harper: Why are 2men and 2women important?

Daniels: The gifts of all of us are greater than the gifts of any one of us. Those who provide support as 2s not only add value to the organization, they add value to those in senior leadership. Their insights, ideas, and encouragement are invaluable. In addition, the support of those who sit in the second chair allows the senior leader or leaders to give the highest and best use of themselves to the organization.

Harper: How difficult is it to find good help?

Daniels: It's very difficult. It has been said that an effective leader must have matches in one hand and a bucket of water in the other. In other words, they must be able to light fires and also put out fires. Those are two essential but different skill sets. It can be challenging to find people who are able to do both.

Finding someone competent can be a bit challenging, but finding someone with chemistry can be even more complex. Chemistry in an organization isn't just about the synergy of personalities; it's also about the alignment of values. If your values don't align, then your chemistry will always be fragile. It can be challenging to find those who have the competence, character, and chemistry needed to provide support. However, challenging doesn't mean impossible; it just means challenging. Therefore, developing people who have 2-level potential is important. If the person has character and chemistry, then competence can be increased if they have capacity.

Harper: One of the greatest investments a 1 could make in the vision is carefully selecting who is going to support him or her. What is the difference between a Joseph and a Joshua?

Daniels: Both serve in support roles—one for a lifetime (Joseph), and the other for a season (Joshua). Joshua was eventually Moses' successor, while Joseph had the ministry of support for a lifetime. Depending on the season a leader is in in the life of the organization determines whether he or she needs to find a Joshua or a Joseph. Chaos, conflict, and catastrophe happen when a leader needs a Joseph but picks a Joshua.

Joshuas should serve in support roles so they can learn responsibility and know what it feels like to carry the weight and bear the burden of leadership. But the Joshuas are going to have a different type of ambition, which can only be harnessed for so long. If the Joshuas aren't mature and emotionally healthy, then that ambition is going to come out in a toxic and potentially disruptive and divisive way.

Josephs have a different type of ambition. They have an ambition that is not for themselves but for the dreams of their pharaohs. Joshuas have their own dreams; Josephs' dreams are intertwined with Pharaoh's. Josephs dream about the dreams of others, and they interpret the dreams of others.

Leaders need to be discerning so they can recognize the Josephs and the Joshuas and the differences between the two. But many leaders, as well as their Joshuas and Josephs, are confused. Some think they are a Joshua but should be a Joseph, or they are a Joseph but should be a Joshua. Senior leaders should not make a decision based on the 2s' perception of who they think they are. Instead, leaders have to make that decision as 1s based on their perceptions of who the Joshuas or Josephs are.

Harper: How does someone in a support role figure out who they are? Am I a Joshua, a Joseph, a Priscilla and Aquila, or a Barnabas?

Daniels: It is possible for people to evolve from one position to another. Josephs may think they will be Josephs for the rest of their lives, and then they enter another season and become Joshuas. This has happened to many people who had no aspirations of being promoted and who didn't think they would ever become more than a Joseph, which proves that many people only have clarity for the season they are in currently.

So what can people do to get clarity on who they are? First, get healthy. I recommend reading *Emotionally Healthy Spirituality: It's Impossible to Be Spiritually Mature, While Remaining Emotionally Immature*, by Peter Scazzero. Read this book, and put into practice the principles Scazzero sets forth. Second, go through grief recovery if you have experienced loss in some form because that grief can have an effect on the way you interpret God's calling on your life. Also read *Emotional Intelligence 2.0*, by Travis Bradberry and Jean Greaves. Their book broaches the patterns and practices of emotionally intelligent people.

As you can see, getting healthy is a step toward discerning who God has called you to be because your needs can often scream louder than God's calling. I've seen people's need for affirmation and importance scream louder than God's calling, and they can confuse all of those issues with their calling.

After you have done those things, then you can be honest with yourself about what your passions are. Are you passionate about supporting; or are you passionate about leading, initiating, mobilizing, building, and gathering? Once you've determined what your passions are, look at what your gifts are. Where are your gifts best served? For example, if someone has a management and strategic gift (administration in the religious sector), then that person should be a 2. But that person has to ask, *Based on my gifts and the way I feel God has called me to display them and distribute them to the world, what is going to be the best role for me to carry them out?* If you ask yourself that question, you should be closer to deciding if you are a Joseph or a Joshua.

Harper: How important is it for a 1 to be emotionally healthy when having a good 2man?

Daniels: The spiritual health (core, character) of 1s is important. They will need Emotional Intelligence (EQ) and Relational Intelligence (RQ), which will help them transform, at best, or manage, at worst, their own issues and insecurities that can be just as toxic to a relationship.

When 2s add value, they are bringing gifts to the table that leaders don't have. So leaders have to be emotionally healthy enough to be secure with what 2s have to offer and emotionally healthy enough to share influence, which is especially important in a religious context.

Relational Intelligence is important for leaders so they will know how to properly manage relationships with their support staff. Everyone is intrinsically equal in that we are all equal in the eyes of God, but we don't all bring equal gifting and equal value to organizations. So when a support leader brings their leaders something rare, gifts and talents that aren't easily replaceable, then leaders have to have the wisdom to handle them correctly and not let those relationships suffer.

Harper: You've mentioned to our staff, and in your advice to other leaders, that senior leaders must value their team as individuals more than they value what they can do. Can you explain what you mean by that?

Daniels: This is simply my personal perspective as a religious leader. I believe that if my priority is caring for the members of my support staff and not just their performance, then everybody wins. The members of my support staff win because they are in an environment where they feel as if they are cared for and are growing and are not just being used for what they can offer. And the organization wins because they are now bringing their best self to the organization.

Harper: You've mentioned that becoming a leader who has character and can be trusted is important. But you've also talked about leaders' commitment to their personal development being critical so that they will never become irrelevant to their staff. Explain.

Daniels: It's what John Maxwell calls "the Law of the Lid." In other words, an organization will never outgrow the lid of the senior leader's leadership acumen. That also applies to a senior leader and a leader who is sitting in the second chair. There is a saying that goes, "No one wants to follow a parked car." If people are interested in growing and developing but are stuck behind leaders who are not interested in growing and developing, then those people will be disillusioned and frustrated. The senior leaders have to make a commitment to grow. If not, they won't be in a position to help, lead, or partner with 2s in carrying out the mission of the organization.

Harper: Years ago, Odell, Derrick, and I discussed the need for a network of some sort that provides coaching, resources, support, and encouragement for 2s like us. One of the things we talked about was seeing great 2s leave their posts to become average 1s. It could have been because of a myriad of things such as ambition, pressure, spousal pressure, fatigue, or even boredom. As a senior leader, have you seen this happen in your own ministry with sons or daughters, or have you seen it happen in other places?

Daniels: Yes, I have seen this happen, and it's a sensitive and controversial issue. Many people in leadership have different ideas of what success looks like, but success is God's best and highest use of a person. Therefore, if that person steps out of position where he or she has been exceptionally proficient and steps into something else where he or she isn't as proficient and fruitful, then it calls into question if God called that person to make that transition at that time.

In Romans 12, Paul says, for example, if your gift is teaching, then teach. If it is leadership, then lead. If your gift is giving, give! In other words, if your gift is giving, then you don't have to teach. Our gifts and calling will not have two different addresses. I'm not saying that we won't be stretched or that people won't need to evolve in their work. I am saying that there are other factors such as external pressure, faulty paradigms, and blind ambition that cause people to step outside of their wheelhouse.

Many people have stepped into pastoral roles because the only paradigms for pastoral ministry in America center around the traditional senior pastor role. The biblical role of pastor is often equated with that of a shepherd. But sometimes the call to pastor is to shepherd people, but it's not a call to shepherd them as a senior pastor. Everyone who is called to shepherd is not necessarily called to be a senior pastor.

People don't have to stay stuck in the structure of an organization their entire lives. But if they step outside of where God has gifted them to be the greatest, then God is probably not the one ordering those steps.

Harper: As a 1, but also as an apostolic father, what are the dangers you see when a person jumps out of his or her set place in an organization?

Daniels: The implications have a ripple effect that the person may not see or be aware of at first. First, the organization is weakened. As Paul describes in 1 Corinthians 12, if the church, or any organization, is like a human body and the members are like body parts, when a body part is missing, then the body is weakened.

Second, the individual is affected, often adversely. When people go from a position where they were highly proficient to one where they're struggling to produce, they may experience economic ramifications for themselves and their families. That's not to mention the emotional and physical toll it can take on people who are in the wrong position. But when they step away from where God called them to be, they are allowing their ambition to lead them; and God doesn't underwrite our ambitions.

CONCLUSION

Do nothing from selfishness or empty conceit [through factional motives, or strife], but with [an attitude of] humility [being neither arrogant nor self-righteous], regard others as more important than yourselves. Do not merely look out for your own personal interests, but also for the interests of others. Have this same attitude in yourselves which was in Christ Jesus [look to Him as your example in selfless humility], who, although He existed in the form and unchanging essence of God [as One with Him, possessing the fullness of all the divine attributes—the entire nature of deity], did not regard equality with God a thing to be grasped or asserted [as if He did not already possess it, or was afraid of losing it]; but emptied Himself [without renouncing or diminishing His deity, but only temporarily giving up the outward expression of divine equality and His rightful dignity] by assuming the form of a bond-servant, and being made in the likeness of men [He became completely human but was without sin, being fully God and fully man]. After He was found in [terms of His] outward appearance as a man [for a divinely-appointed time], He humbled Himself [still further] by becoming obedient [to the Father] to the point of death, even death on a cross. For this reason also [because He obeyed and so completely humbled Himself], God has highly exalted Him and bestowed on Him the name which is above every name. (Philippians 2:3-9, Amplified Bible)

Philippians 2:3-9 is the theological thought behind this book. This Scripture passage gives a spiritual foundation to help us understand that no one man is an island unto himself. In order for your organization, team, or ministry to be successful, someone has to be willing to decrease. Remember, 1s and 2s are not in competition but are on the same team working toward the same goal.

I hope that this book has been beneficial to executive support leaders (2s) as well as to senior leaders (1s). The partnership between a senior leader and his 2man is critical not only in order to help advance the kingdom of God but also in order to strengthen our companies and organizations. I believe that helping people understand their unique calling and purpose allows them the ability to serve with clarity.

The qualities required to have longevity and success were outlined in this book by those who have been fruitful and successful in their 2men roles for many years. They are well acquainted with how their positions affect their families and the other unique challenges 2s face. I pray that the advice given will prove helpful. I also hope "Things 2s Want 1s to Know" and the interview with Dr. Dharius Daniels prove beneficial because you will see that you are not alone in your role and discover that many of the things you have been thinking and feeling are common to many others.

More importantly, I pray that this resource inspires you to want to be part of a network of like-minded leaders, which is why we have established www.2mansupport.com. Remember, like the dynamic hip hop duo shared in 1988, "It takes 2 to make it outta sight!"

ABOUT THE AUTHOR

Ramone Harper

Ramone is the founder of BNB Consulting and Associates, a management and consulting firm that contracts with ministries, organizations, not-for-profits, and start-ups in the areas of business organization and development, staff and leadership development, and branding. He also serves as executive pastor at Change Church in Ewing, New Jersey, where he oversees all ministry operations and campus pastors and assists the lead pastor to interpret and strategically execute goals and objectives.

In 2016, Ramone co-authored the book *It Was All a Dream*, of which 100 percent of the proceeds go toward the Turning Dreams Into Realities (www.tdi2r.org) scholarship and mentoring nonprofit organization, where he serves as a founder and a board member.

Ramone earned his BS in public relations with a minor in business administration from Alabama State University, where he graduated summa cum laude in 1997. He is currently enrolled at Regents University, working on his master of divinity degree. Recently, he was selected as one of the Ebony Men of the Year by Alpha Kappa Alpha Sorority, Inc., included in the 2013-2015 *Who's Who in Black Houston* publication as one of the top entrepreneurs, and honored as one of Houston's Top 50 Entrepreneurs in 2015.

Ramone is originally from Detroit, Michigan, but lived the majority of his teenage years in the Dallas-Fort Worth area. He is married to his life partner, Verily, and they have four children (Ilexuz, Amari, Raven, Ziy'hon) and one grandchild (the young prince Deon).

CONTRIBUTORS

Dr. Dharius Daniels

Dharius Daniels is a cultural architect and trendsetter for his generation. He is an innovative leader, strategic thinker, and articulate and prolific preacher. In August 2005, he became the founder and senior pastor of Change Church (formerly Kingdom Church). With one location in Ewing, New Jersey, and another in Westampton, New Jersey, this is a vibrant ministry that impacts people of all ages and socioeconomic and ethnic backgrounds.

Pastor Daniels has developed a breathtaking ministry concept that describes the standard of excellence at Change Church: a standard that is apparent in his commitment not only to ministry but also to education.

Pastor Daniels holds a bachelor of arts degree in political science from Millsaps College in Jackson, Mississippi; a master of divinity degree from Princeton Theological Seminary in Princeton, New Jersey; and a doctorate of ministry degree from Fuller Theological Seminary in Pasadena, California. He has a versatile gift and speaks frequently in seminaries and churches across the country.

Verily Harris-Harper, LPC, NCC

Verily has found a way to combine over 16 years of professional and clinical experience. And her diverse experiences are described as nothing short of amazing, because good or bad, her perspective is that they were necessary and valuable aspects of the journey. What Verily was able to discover was paramount because she realized that the "best life" is an inside job. The "best life" begins with the "best self," and it is out of this discovery that TBE Global LLC was formed. The recipe is quite simple: "Small change, BIG IMPACT."

Verily graduated magna cum laude with a bachelor's degree in business management from LeTourneau University in Longview, Texas, and graduated with highest honors with a master's degree in mental health counseling from Capella University. Verily is a Nationally Certified Counselor licensed in Texas and New Jersey.

Olus R. Holder Jr., MDiv
Executive Pastor, Fallbrook Church, Houston, Texas
Pastor: Pastor Michael A. Pender Sr.

Cheryletta "C. C." Harrison
CEO, The City of Love Church, New Orleans, Louisiana
Pastor: Bishop Lester Love

Layne Schranz
Associate Pastor, Church of the Highlands,
Multiple campuses throughout Alabama
Pastor: Pastor Chris Hodges

Derrick D. Noble Sr.
Chief of Staff to the Presiding Bishop,
Full Gospel Baptist Church Fellowship International
Nashville, Tennessee
Pastor: Bishop Joseph W. Walker III

Corbett Drew
Executive Director, Venue Church, Chattanooga, Tennessee
Pastor: Pastor Tavner Smith

Phil Clemens
Global Executive Team Operations Pastor / Campus Pastor,
Faith Church, St. Louis, Missouri
Pastors: Pastors Keith and Nicole Crank

WHAT YOU CAN EXPECT FROM 2MANSUPPORT.COM

In preparation for launching this book and this organization, I did a lot of research to find out if anything like it already existed. I would like to acknowledge the incredible work that people like Beverly Robinson and Marjorie Duncan have done in developing the CEASE organization (www.ceaseadmin.com), which is designed to provide support to executive administrative assistants and on whose advisory board I have the pleasure of serving.

I want to thank authors Mike Bonem and Roger Patterson (*Leading From the Second Chariot*); Jacquetta Smith (*Loyalty: The Pathway to Promotion*); and one of the best 2s that I have ever met, Mr. Terry Nance (*God's Armor Bearer*), who I reference often in this book. I read books such as *Consiglieri*, by Richard Hytner, which captures the essence and spirit of a 2man in the corporate world. Richard did a great job in helping show the similarities that exist between a senior leader and his 2, the differences in their leadership styles, the types of 2s, and advice for each of these important leaders.

I won't try to restate what they wrote; but with this resource and corresponding coaching network (www.2mansupport.com), I'm attempting to pick up where they left off. I wanted to provide insight into the minds of 2s from one who has served in that capacity for many years for various leaders; give insight on the value and perspective from senior leaders who are the recipients of 2s' support but who have had to lead for various seasons without a capable 2; and to provide support, resources, and mentoring (which, to me, is the greatest missing link) to the many called, chosen, and sometimes hesitant 2s who are out there.

BIBLIOGRAPHY

Consiglieri: Leading From the Shadows, by Richard Hytner (Profile Books, 2014).

God's Armor Bearer: Serving God's Leaders, revised edition, by Terry Nance (Spirit-Filled Books, 2003). Nance served 23 years with Agape Church in Little Rock, Arkansas, as the senior associate and executive director of Agape Missionary Alliance. He is now president of Focus on the Harvest Ministries.
"Horse," Wikipedia (https://en.m.wikipedia.org/wiki/Horse).
How to Lead When You're Not in Charge, by Clay Scroggins (Zondervan, 2017) (https://itunes.apple.com/us/book/how-to-lead-when-youre-not-in-charge/id1201977209?mt=11).
Leading From the Second Chair: Serving Your Church, Fulfilling Your Role, and Realizing Your Dreams, by Mike Bonem and Roger Patterson (Jossey-Bass, 2005).
Loyalty: The Pathway to Promotion, Working Up Close and Personal in Ministry, by Jacquetta Brown Smith (VJS Productions, Inc. 2003). Smith served as executive director at New Light Christian Center in Houston, Texas, under the leadership of Dr. I. V. Hilliard.

RePresent Jesus: Rethink Your Version of Christianity and Become More Like Christ, by Dharius Daniels (Charisma House, 2014).

"Second in Command: The Misunderstood Role of the Chief Operating Officer," by Nathan Bennett and Stephen Miles for *Harvard Business Review*, May 2006 (https://hbr.org/2006/05/second-in-command-the-misunderstood-role-of-the-chief-operating-officer).

Shoulder to Shoulder: Strengthening Your Church by Supporting Your Pastor, by Dan Reiland (Thomas Nelson, 1997). Reiland is vice president of leadership and church development at INJOY.

The Associate Pastor: Second Chair, Not Second Best, by Martin E. Hawkins (B&H Books, 2005). Hawkins served as associate pastor for 29 years alongside Dr. Tony Evans at Oak Cliff Bible Fellowship in Dallas, Texas.

The Emotionally Healthy Leader: How Transforming Your Inner Life Will Deeply Transform Your Church, Team, and the World, by Peter Scazzero (Zondervan, 2015).

The Enemies of Excellence: 7 Reasons Why We Sabotage, by Greg Cachi (The Crossroad Publishing Company, 2011).

www.ingramcontent.com/pod-product-compliance
Lightning Source LLC
Chambersburg PA
CBHW021118210326
41598CB00017B/1484